# Listening Counts:
## listening to young learners of mathematics

# Listening Counts:
## listening to young learners of mathematics

*Edited by*
*Jenny Houssart and John Mason*

**Trentham Books**

Stoke on Trent, UK and Sterling, USA

# UNIVERSITY OF CHICHESTER

Trentham Books Limited
Westview House      22883 Quicksilver Drive
734 London Road    Sterling
Oakhill             VA 20166-2012
Stoke on Trent      USA
Staffordshire
England ST4 5NP

First published 2009

British Library Cataloguing-in-Publication Data
A catalogue record for this book is available from the British Library

ISBN: 978 1 85856 448 7

Designed and typeset by Trentham Print Design Ltd, Chester and printed in Great Britain by Page Bros (Norwich) Ltd.

## Acknowledgements
We would like to thank all the children who feature in the accounts presented in this book. The editors would also like to thank all those who helped in putting the book together.

A few of the incidents reported by Dave Hewitt in chapter 1 were previously published in *Mathematics Teaching*. Some of the incidents drawn on in chapter 5 appeared in *Low Attainers in Primary Mathematics* by Jenny Houssart published by Routledge Falmer. In both cases, we are grateful for permission to reproduce them. The material in chapter 8 draws on a joint research project between the Centre for Mathematics Education at the Open University, the Qualifications and Curriculum Authority and Edexcel. We are grateful to all those who participated in this project. The material in chapter 11 is reproduced with permission of Curtis Brown Group Ltd, London, on behalf of the Trustees of the Mass Observation Archive Copyright © The Trustees of the Mass Observation Archive.

Cover picture: *Alice listens to her son, Joe, explaining the rules of his new game. Photograph by Hilary Evens with permission from Alice Fox*

# Contents

**Introduction** • vii
*Jenny Houssart and John Mason*

Chapter 1
**From before birth to beginning school** • 1
*Dave Hewitt*

Chapter 2
**'There are numbers in Australia': young children's
perceptions of number and shape** • 17
*Nichola Abraham*

Chapter 3
**Young children and adults listening and working
mathematically together** • 31
*Hilary Evens*

Chapter 4
**Listening matters** • 45
*Mary Briggs*

Chapter 5
**Unofficial talk in mathematics classrooms** • 59
*Jenny Houssart*

Chapter 6
**Matchbox algebra** • 71
*Alan Graham and Roger Duke*

Chapter 7

**Learning to add fractions: a progression of experiences or an experience of the progression?** • 85

*Andreas O. Kyriakides*

Chapter 8

**Can more be learned from interviews than from written answers?** • 101

*Hilary Evens and Jenny Houssart*

Chapter 9

**Pupils' perception of setting** • 115

*Barbara Allen*

Chapter 10

**'Listen, it's easy': children as teachers of counting** • 127

*Brian Dale, Elizabeth Ryder, Lisa Strong, Jenny Houssart*

Chapter 11

**Latter day reflections on primary mathematics** • 143

*Jenny Houssart*

Chapter 12

**Learning from listening to yourself** • 157

*John Mason*

**Notes on contributors** • 171

**Author Index** • 173

**Subject Index** • 175

# Introduction

## Jenny Houssart and John Mason

### Listening to learners of mathematics

The overall question addressed by this book is 'What can be learned by listening to young learners of mathematics?' In the following chapters, a range of authors share their research, reflection on their own practice or experience with children. Different approaches and perspectives are adopted, but all the authors are hoping to learn something from this listening, and to make use of what they learn. We advocate listening to learners not as an add-on, but as an integral part of the teaching and learning of mathematics. Indeed we follow Brent Davis (1996) in his suggestion that it is possible to teach through listening, not exclusively but significantly. We believe that all those who work alongside children working on mathematics inside or outside of classrooms can gain insight and inform their future practice by using this approach.

### Definitions of listening

Many of the chapters in this book concern what children say whilst engaged in learning and doing mathematics and what they say about mathematics. However, we also wish to look beyond the spoken word and to use a range of other evidence. This is partly because of the age of the children involved, which suggests that a wide definition of listening is appropriate. The nature of the subject also supports this view, allowing us to take into account children's calculations, diagrams and actions while working on mathematics. Early chapters in particular draw on approaches to listening advocated in early childhood education (eg Rinaldi, 2008). Thus we see listening as being open to the thoughts and ideas of others.

Another key issue when it comes to listening to children is whether any-thing happens as a result. McLeod (2008) points out that the literature on listening to children includes writers who define listening in terms of attitude and those who take it to imply action. The second type of listening is supported by a recent report on primary mathematics (Williams, 2008), which stresses the importance of listening as part of discussion in primary mathematics classrooms and draws on a recent review of literature advocating transformative listening (Kyriacou and Issit, 2008). This is said to take place when teachers listen to pupils' con-tributions in a way that suggests a genuine meeting of minds and the teacher's willingness to change their thinking in the light of what the pupil has said.

We adopt a definition of listening which draws on a range of informa-tion and is followed by action. However, we suggest that although action may be immediate, this is not always the case and there is often an intermediate step of interpretation, which can be far from straight-forward (Wallach and Even, 2005). This leads us to a three step model of listening which involves:

- openness to information, verbal and otherwise, from learners,
- consideration of possible interpretation of this information and
- action based on this information.

This was the model we used when putting together this collection of chapters. Contributors were encouraged to write data rich chapters which were based around accounts or quotes obtained by listening, or paying attention to learners of mathematics. As a second stage, the authors were asked to consider what we might learn from these accounts, and what to do with what we learn. Our main emphasis throughout is on teaching and learning mathematics and the information-interpretation-action cycle will often directly concern mathematical understanding, though it will also sometimes concern issues that impact on this understanding, such as preferred ways of learning.

## Approaches to listening

The accounts in this book were obtained in three ways: listening as an integral part of working with children; task-based interviews used to research children's mathematical understanding and consultation on children's perspectives. In many cases, the lines between these three approaches are blurred.

## Listening to learning

Four chapters lead with the idea of listening carefully to children as they go about learning and doing mathematics. In the first chapter Dave Hewitt discusses his experience of listening to his young daughters at home before they were school-age. Dave necessarily adopts a wide view of listening, considering a range of evidence including the physical actions of his daughters when they were very young. From each incident he draws messages which have informed his approach to teaching mathematics to older students. Hilary Evens also listens to children going about mathematics: in her case the children are part of a family numeracy group and she is the tutor. Whilst working in this role Hilary kept a diary to record particular incidents and she draws on some of these to consider what they tell us about the children in the group. Hilary is concerned with a range of listening combinations such as children listening to each other, adults listening to children, adults listening to each other.

Two of the chapters about older primary children are based in mathematics classrooms. Andreas Kyriakides writes as a teacher researcher describing in detail how his class responded to a lesson on fractions. Key themes of his chapter are how students listen to each other and how listening to his students has impacted on the way he teaches. Jenny Houssart writes as a researcher who adopts a role similar to a classroom assistant. Her focus is on unofficial talk in classes of children who are considered to be low-attainers in mathematics. She asks what we can learn about their mathematical understanding from this unofficial talk and wonders why children choose to make comments in this way. Some of the comments are about preferred approaches to mathematics and like several other chapters this looks at pupil perspectives through an observational approach.

## Task-based interviews

Two of the chapters are derived from a clinical interview approach which is designed to consider children's understanding of particular aspects of mathematics, although this approach is much adapted. Alan Graham and Roger Duke record the responses of pupils working on prototype computer software which is designed to introduce early algebra. Their chapter focuses mostly on mathematical understanding, but also deals with pupil preferences. A key point of the chapter is that there is a good reason for seeking pupils' views at the design stage of the software. Hilary Evens and Jenny Houssart continue the early algebraic theme and base their chapter on interviews carried out with pairs of children. Again, the focus is on mathematical understanding but the authors also try to compare information gained from interviews with written information and to consider the impact of interviewing children in pairs.

## Pupil perspectives

Barbara Allen's chapter deals directly with pupil perspectives and is based on a series of interviews designed to gain their views of a range of issues in teaching and learning mathematics. Barbara focuses on pupils' views of the practice of setting, which involves teaching pupils with similar attainment together for mathematics. Two other chapters also consider pupil perspectives alongside other approaches. Nichola Abraham explores nursery children's perceptions of number and shape. She draws on the mosaic approach often used to obtain the perspectives of young pupils, but combines this with a more mathematical focus, using questions about number and shape alongside the use of a digital camera (Clark and Moss, 2001). Mary Briggs uses a range of approaches in her chapter, including classroom observation and discussions with children about how and why they use number.

## Other interpretations of listening

The final three chapters take more unusual approaches. Brian Dale, Elizabeth Ryder and Lisa Strong consider their experience of learning to count in a new language with the assistance of children. Their accounts are explored to consider issues about teaching and learning and about different number systems. The next chapter draws on written accounts by older adults which shed light on their perceptions of their primary mathematics education received many years earlier. Some indicate that their views of primary mathematics have changed as a result of later experiences, for example as a primary teacher or a grandparent. Finally,

John Mason invites readers to listen to themselves while engaged in mathematical tasks. He also suggests the use of a diary as part of this approach.

## Summary

One of the emerging themes from the chapters is that children are eager to express themselves and their mathematical thinking, as long as the conditions are supportive and non-judgemental. When there is a relaxed atmosphere in which everything that is said and done is seen as a conjecture which is thought about and modified when necessary and when everyone listens respectfully to each other, fruitful and productive discussion ensues.

## References

Clark, A and Moss, P (2001) *Listening to Young Children, The Mosaic Approach.* London: National Children's Bureau and Joseph Rowntree Foundation

Davis, B (1996) *Teaching Mathematics: Towards a sound alternative.* New York: Ablex

Kyriacou, C and Issit, J (2008) *What characterises effective teacher-initiated teacher-pupil dialogue to promote conceptual understanding in mathematics lessons in key stages 2 and 3: a systematic review.* London: Eppi-Centre Social Science Research Unit, Institute of Education, University of London

McLeod, A (2008) *Listening to Children: A Practitioner's Guide.* London: Jessica Kingsley Publishers

Rinaldi, C (2008) Documentation and assessment: what is the relationship? In A. Clark, A. Kjorholt and P. Moss (eds) *Beyond Listening: Children's Perspectives on Early Childhood Services.* Bristol: The Policy Press

Wallach, T and Even, R (2005) Hearing students: the complexity of understanding what they are saying, showing, and doing. *Journal of Mathematics Teacher Education* 8 p393-417

Williams, P (2008) *Independent Review of Mathematics Teaching in Early Years Settings and Primary Schools: Final Report.* Nottingham: DCSF Publications

# 1

# From before birth to beginning school
## *Dave Hewitt*

I am an ex-secondary teacher and head of mathematics who has now worked in initial teacher education as well as with experienced secondary teachers of mathematics on Masters degree courses. My practice as a teacher of both teenagers and adults has been informed by listening to young children, often of pre-school age, and considering how they go about the impressive learning they achieve. This chapter focuses on incidents which I have heard or observed involving my daughters who, at the time of writing, are 4 and 7 years old, mainly whilst they were of pre-school age, and how reflection upon those incidents has implications for my professional practice as a teacher of primary, secondary or adult students. The choice of reporting observations of my own daughters is particular, but the events described are exemplars of general activity with which all children engage. I invite the reader to consider memories and experiences which may be evoked from reading these reports and to see what can be learned with regard to our practice as teachers, parents and guardians.

These events are not in chronological order but in an order which builds upon pedagogical issues. So when I mention Danya, the elder girl or Tamsin, the younger, I give their ages in brackets at the time of the event.

## Event 1

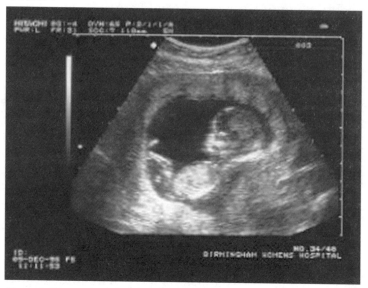

Figure 1: Danya aged negative six months

I was lucky to watch both my daughters move in their mother's womb through the technology of a scan. With Danya (negative 6 months) I observed her pushing her feet against the side of the womb (see figure 1). This made her body slide up higher in the womb, and then her body would slide down again until the next push. This seemed to be a great opportunity for Danya to learn something about the effect of pushing with her feet. She had a level of control over her leg muscles and this requires learning to have taken place. I have no idea about whether she did learn anything or not on the occasion I observed. However, her actions appeared deliberate and similar to those she made later several months after being born when she pushed her feet against a wall when she was on her back and was trying to reach something.

## Reflection 1

Children engage with their environment and developing skills well before they are born. Sometimes this can be ignored – as if learning only starts after someone is born and that no skills have been developed already. There is an incorrect image of a newborn child as an empty vessel, which is a denial of the learning and skills already developed.

Likewise, as a teacher there is a danger that I do not consider the relevance of the previous experiences of my students when I come to teach a topic and do not make use of existing skills which have been developed. I could treat a student as an empty vessel who has no experiences of relevance to what I am about to teach.

## Event 2

Danya (11 months) used to sit on the floor and throw things out of her reach. She would then complain that she could not reach them. Yet she was not interested in the object if I fetched it for her.

## Reflection 2

Danya did not seem to be interested in the object as much as the activity of trying to reach it. Initially I thought she wanted the object which was now out of reach but I suggest that she deliberately threw it so that it was out of reach. She became good at reaching as far as possible without actually crawling, which she was one month away from achieving. Trying to get something which is out of reach is a great challenge which can develop new ways in which Danya can use her body to extend her reach and this can lead to her being able to crawl. More generally, I am aware that young children do not seem that interested in things they can do easily. They seem to want to do things which require a skill beyond their current mastery. Both my girls wanted to turn a key in a lock when they could not do it; they wanted to pour milk in their cereal when it would spill all over the table; they wanted to stack a set of cups into a tower when it would keep falling over. And once a skill had been achieved it seemed no longer of interest. I recall that after Danya had learnt to stack her set of cups she would then try to do so whilst holding a felt lollipop in one hand and a felt flower in the other. Once one challenge was within her reach she would set herself a new one which was once again beyond her reach.

So what do I offer my students in a classroom? Do I offer them something which is within their reach? There can be a desire to offer students something which they can do. After all, if students cannot do what is set there can be management issues to deal with. Yet young children seem to want to try to do things which they cannot do. They get frustrated but that does not change the fact that this is the kind of challenge they set themselves. I suggest it is also the way in which children learn to extend their current skills. If they are only practising skills already obtained, little new is learned. Learning is about extending oneself, being in a state of becoming about to do something which could not be done before, or acquiring a new way of seeing something which makes sense when previously it all seemed random and chaotic. The metaphor of Danya deliberately wanting something beyond her current reach helped me to consider what I offer my students. I want to offer something which is not immediately achievable, which requires them to extend themselves beyond their current skill level. I know that Danya would not be interested if the object was so far away from her that it was impossible to get. Ideally it would be just beyond her reach so that she would need to do something different from what she has done before in order to extend her reach further. Likewise, I don't want to offer something which is impossible for my students to achieve. I want to offer something which is tantalisingly just out of reach, something which can be conceived as do-able but which will require a different response, not just a repetition of what is already familiar. My students will get frustrated.

The issue for me is not to respond to such frustrations by offering something easier which is within their grasp but to support them during these times of frustration. One way to do this is to prepare students beforehand, to announce that the set task is a challenge and that there will be times when they feel frustrated. Another is to discuss what strategies they might use when they do get frustrated.

As an example for some students who are just beginning to feel confident with finding area, I offer the shift from finding areas of squares such as in Figure 2, to finding areas of squares as in Figure 3.

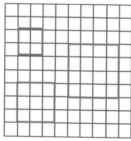
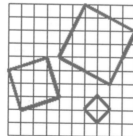

Figure 2          Figure 3

## Event 3

When talking about whose certain things were, I noticed that Danya (2 years 3 months) was saying 'Mummy's' and 'Daddy's' but she was also saying 'Mine's'.

## Reflection 3

'Mine's' is not usually said and so it stuck out. However, the fact that it is unusual is not always sufficient for me to take particular note of it. In this case I brought with me, as part of my own experiences, an interest in the way young children learn language rules when these are rarely explicitly taught. So the reason I noticed this event and made a note of it on paper was as much to do with my own interests as with the event itself. John Mason (2002) would say I had not just noticed but also marked the event. I bring with me, as we all do, a collection of past experiences and issues of interest, whether conscious or unconscious. It is the meeting of an event along with these personal experiences and issues where the two relate in some way. So an event in itself only becomes significant for a particular individual or collection of individuals, because of their own experiences and interests. This event for me is an example of how children abstract a rule which fits examples they have heard and begin applying that rule in new situations. For others it may be an event which shows other things, such as how our schools are not teaching children to speak properly! So my first reflection is concerned with the creation of significance being formed out of a coming together of a particular person with their particular personal interests and experiences and the event itself.

Further reflection was about the details of my own interest. Danya was never told there is a rule about adding an -s on the end of a possessive words or pronouns. But she has heard many examples, such as mummy's, daddy's, his, hers, its, which all seem to end with an s sound. So Danya saying 'mine's' indicates to me that she has established that rule, whether consciously or unconsciously, as she cannot have copied this. So she must be applying a rule herself and applying it to new situations which she has not heard before since she will never have heard 'mine's'. The problem with the English language is that there are so many exceptions to rules – how is someone to know about exceptions? The son of a friend of mine came home from his London school almost in tears when he was about 5 years old, saying that it is all too hard when he found out that but and put are pronounced so differently. Young children are good at abstracting rules and applying them to new situations. They have to do this in order to learn their first language. Exceptions have to be learnt one by one, since they are exceptions to a rule. This is why young children learn that you put -ed at the end of a verb in order to talk about the past and apply this rule to most verbs, including exceptions. As I recall, Danya and Tamsin began saying things like 'I threwed the ball' when they were about 3 years old, which means that they had abstracted this rule by that time. However, Danya still occasionally adds -ed onto the end of verbs which are exceptions to this rule even now when she is 7 years and 3 months old. Abstracting a rule is relatively easy compared with memorising all the exceptions.

In mathematics there are many examples of students applying rules to inappropriate situations. For example, *two negatives make a positive* might be misapplied to the sum -3 + -2 to get +5 . They have learnt a rule and remembering a rule is one thing but knowing when that rule does or does not apply often involves greater complexity. This is particularly so when a mathematical rule is told to students as something to memorise. A student may succeed in memorising the rule but applying it only to appropriate mathematical situations is not easy without a sense of the mathematics underlying the rule. I represent this situation in Figure 4, where the student tries to memorise the rule but the mathematical situation for which the rule applies has got left behind. A teacher may think that all is fine if the rule is successfully memorised when in fact a student may have little idea of the mathematics relating to that rule.

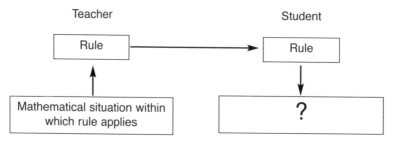

Figure 4: a student can become distanced from mathematics if the task is to memorise given rules

An alternative is represented in Figure 5, where the student is immersed in the mathematical situation and from it tries to establish a general rule. A teacher may start with a syllabus and decide that there is a rule that students should know, but instead of telling the students about the rule, a relevant mathematical situation is offered to them from which the rule can be abstracted. Students have spent their life abstracting rules such as the grammatical rules of language, and this is an important part of mathematics. In this way a student remains in touch with not only the mathematically relevant situation but also acts as a mathematician in trying to establish patterns and rules associated with that situation.

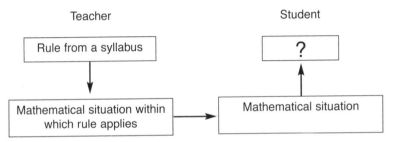

Figure 5: a student stays in touch with the mathematics

So the task for a teacher shifts from explaining rules clearly and helping students memorise, to finding an activity from which students can abstract the desired rule. For example, with *two negatives make a positive*, I might offer the following activity:

Put several numbers into a bubble and write down an expression to represent their total if added together:

$$3 + {}^-2 + 7 + 1 = 9$$

Figure 6

Then consider adding extra numbers into the bubble or taking them away. The key issue is taking away a negative number such as the -2 and writing what has been done. Having started with 9 since we already know the total from before, we take away the -2, and so write 9 – -2. This leaves 11 which is obtained from looking at which numbers are left in the bubble and adding them up:

$$9 - {}^-2 = 11$$

Figure 7

Such activities can lead to students developing their own rule for what happens when a negative number is taken away.

Some students may not abstract the rule and only meet it when other students report discovering this rule. In such situations the students will at least be far more familiar with the mathematical situation to which the rule applies.

## Event 4

Danya (3yrs 9m) was wearing a dress with three pockets, one at the top and two lower down and she told me she had a pocket in her dress. Then she looked down further and said she had two more pockets. I asked her 'and how many does that make?' She looked at me and said 'You know that!'

## Reflection 4

Indeed I did know that. There is a difference between an honest question where there is something I do not know and want to know, and a pedagogic question, where the question is used as a tool in an attempt to help someone with their learning. Children can often spot the difference. How often in my classroom do I ask honest questions? I suspect that most of my questions are pedagogic in nature. However, there are times when I ask honest questions and I classify these into two types in the next paragraphs.

There are questions where I ask about the mathematics I am teaching, such as what is 12+27? or what is the third angle of an isosceles triangle if two of the angles are 53 and 74? These mathematical questions are ones to which I know the answer. However, there are questions where I do not ask about the mathematics but about a person, such as how did you work out 12+27? or How did you know the third angle was 53? Here my question is an honest one as I really do not know how this particular student worked out this problem and do want to find out. This is the first type of honest question I ask where I learn about my students. Watson (2006) suggests a shift in questioning,

> changing 'do you understand X?' to 'what do you understand about X?' which signals a shift from students telling you about something you know to your listening to what they know. (p42)

This turns a pedagogic question into an honest question and shifts attention onto learning about learners.

The second type of honest question I ask is about the mathematics. In this case it is not so much about some mathematics content, which is on the syllabus, but a particular mathematical problem. For example, I know a certain amount about fractions and about adding fractions, but I do not know the answer to the question: 'how many ways can you write the fraction $\frac{11}{13}$ as a sum of fractions that all have 1 as their numerator, which are often referred to as Egyptian fractions?' I know that I could answer this question but sometimes I choose to bring the problem into the classroom so that we can all look at it together. Then when a student has an insight into this question it is an honest and genuine surprise to me and I can learn about mathematics from my students as much as they can learn mathematics from me. I am still a teacher and have certain knowledge which can help students in their learning.

For example, I can assist students in a variety of ways, such as helping them understand the question, helping those who have difficulty adding fractions, who have found one solution but are not sure how to look for another and who are trying to justify why there are no more solutions. I can also help by listening and asking students to be clear and articulate about what they are saying, using appropriate mathematical language. There are many teaching roles I can take on which are different from telling students an answer or how to do the problem.

I do not even need to know at the time how to actually solve the problem – this is the students' challenge. My challenge is to attend to the students and their mathematical thinking. I need to know enough mathematics to be able to recognise when the problem has or has not been solved by a student. This does not mean that I carry the answer in my head: if I did, it would no longer be an honest question. Instead I need to know enough about mathematics to know that when I listen to what a student tells me I can decide whether what they are saying is mathematically correct or not. In this case, to answer the question fully requires an element of proof and so I need to be able to decide whether I am mathematically convinced by an argument which a student might present. Even then I may decide that I will not be the initial judge of such an argument. I might decide to ask other students to listen to the argument and see whether they agree or whether there is a flaw in the argument. Thus it is not only myself as teacher who listens to learners but also other learners are expected to listen to each other.

## Event 5

Tamsin (4 yrs and 2 mths) was involved in some role play. As she was pretending to make me a cup of tea she said, 'It will be ready in about five hours'.

## Reflection 5

Sometimes listening to one event can trigger a recall of other events as well. This was the case for me with this incident. I recalled a time when Tamsin was talking about what she wanted to do in a day and she said, 'After we have had lunch at about eight o'clock...'. Then another time, when we were role playing going shopping, she said that something like a carrot would cost me one hundred and twenty pounds. Sometimes seeming separate incidents can begin to come together and a common thread begins to link them. This was the case for me as these incidents came to mind and then, a little later after the cup of tea incident, Tamsin sold me a pretend flower and told me it would cost me one thousand pence.

On reflection I was initially taken by these incidents because the numbers were so far away from a realistic value. It was endearing! Yet as these incidents came together in my mind I realised that what was really significant was that Tamsin was using appropriate units after these numbers. The link for me between these events was units. Not that long ago Tamsin would say something like 'that is a long pencil, it is about 24 hours'. Tamsin was now finding opportunities in her role play to say units in a context and check out whether they were accepted by others in that context. When we talk about when something happens, do we say '... o'clock'? When we talk about how long something takes, do we say 'hours'? When we say how much something costs, do we say 'pence'? Or do we say 'pounds'? When would we say 'pence' and when would we say 'pounds'? This is all quite difficult for a child to work out, particularly when they are not being told these things explicitly.

I realised that there was a hierarchy. First Tamsin concerned herself with numbers, saying numbers and trying to find out what is a big number and what is not a big number. Along with Danya, we used to tell each other how much we loved each other in terms of a number. At one time Tamsin said 'I love you one billion hours ... [pause] ... Dad, is that a big number?' She is learning number names and, as well as learning the name, there is also the issue of whether that name represents a big number or not. So attention is on learning number names first and then learning the relative values associated with those names. I will ignore the issue of learning the symbols associated with that number name.

Then there is a stage when Tamsin realised that units are sometimes said after a number name. She was already aware of that when she made the statement '.. one billion hours'. The awareness that units exist and that they are said after a number comes before realising which units are said within which context. So there are two stages within the learning of saying appropriate units.

Finally there is a shift of attention back onto numbers as Tamsin begins to consider what number might be appropriate to use within the context and chosen units. So when she tells me that a pretend flower I want to buy from her shop will cost me three hundred pounds, it might be useful for her if I say 'Hmmm ... that is an expensive flower.'

So there is a hierarchy in learning about units:

- saying number names and getting an idea of relative size of numbers
- saying a unit name at the end of a number

■  saying an appropriate unit given the context

■  using appropriately sized numbers for those units and context

As with most learning, this hierarchy is unlikely to run in order so that exploration of saying a unit only comes after the an idea of the relative size of numbers has been mastered. These stages often overlap and run in parallel. For example, Tamsin's mention of '... one billion hours ...' occurred four months after the original incident where I realised Tamsin was using appropriate units. Just because she has sorted out when some units are said does not mean she has sorted out all of them. Likewise, just because she has learnt the relative size of many numbers does not mean she knows the relative size of all possible number names. Yet a hierarchy does exist in that:

1.  a child starts by learning number names although there are other hierarchies which lead to this but I need to start somewhere, and so attention is on number names

2.  some number names need to be known before the child can begin to compare relative sizes of numbers: attention is on size

3.  some number names have to be known before the child can say a unit name after saying a number: attention is on units

4.  some unit names have to be known and used before the child can choose which unit name should be said in a particular context: attention is on contexts

5.  some suitable combinations of contexts and units need to be known in order to decide on an appropriate sized number to use: attention is on size of numbers in relation to particular units in particular contexts.

The awareness of this hierarchy informs my actions in relation to other areas of the mathematics curriculum where units are used. For example, work across different dimensions such as length, area and volume brings up the issue of whether units are linear, squared or cubed. This issue becomes a focus for many students. Also, when information is given about a problem in different units, such as some lengths are in cm and others in mm, a problem might require a student to decide upon a common unit. So as a teacher, I might be pleased that students use appropriate units in certain contexts before worrying about particular numerical values or estimations. In fact, it could be fun to use inappropriate numbers when I am clear that my teaching focus is on the choice of unit: this can help someone who is not confident because they have made a poor estimate. Later on they may become confident about saying the appropriate unit and attention is then placed on the size of the number of those units. In fact, at this stage the focus on appropriate size of numbers requires the student to become familiar with the unit itself. For example, exactly how long is a metre? It is no good trying to estimate a length in metres or judge the appropriateness of an answer without a sense of how long one metre actually is. Even though attention was on the unit in stage 3, and to some extent in stage 4, it was mainly on the socially agreed name of the unit, rather than its size. It is only when attention returns to the number and its appropriate size that attention goes back to the nature of the unit itself. At this point I need an image which helps me to understand the size of a unit such as a metre. Benchmarks, such as the height of a door being roughly two metres, offer an image from which I can judge the appropriateness of the numbers of that unit.

The issue of a possible hierarchy, and so a potential change in my focus as a teacher, might appear in other areas of the curriculum to units. For example, I might be pleased that a learner knows the word division and can say it correctly. On another occasion I would be pleased that a learner recognises that to solve a particular problem might involve division. At yet another time I might be looking for appropriate numbers to be involved in that division: for example, three cereal bars being divided between six people involves $3 \div 6$ and not $6 \div 3$. And still another time I want someone to be able to carry out a division correctly. Considering such hierarchies can help me to plan an approach to a topic which will recognise and involve progression. It can help me be aware that even if someone does not get a answer to a problem correct, they might show success at other levels within that hierarchy. It can help me decide on the focus for a particular learner. It can help me become aware of the fact that learning is a complex activity!

## Event 6

I was with Danya (6yrs 3m) and Tamsin on Branscombe beach, which is stony. It was a cold day and after filling the bucket a few times, Danya said she was getting bored. I said that I bet she couldn't cover up my arm with stones as she had done previously with sand. She and Tamsin became motivated and started digging and filling their buckets fast and pouring them over my arm.

## Reflection 6

At first Danya showed interest in filling up her bucket with stones but that interest only lasted so long. The renewed interest only came when filling a bucket with stones was not the focus of attention in itself but related to a new project: covering my arms with stones, which used the filling of the bucket as a step on the way. This raises the nature of practice and how I can organise my students to practise a skill in which I want them to become fluent. I can offer a sheet with plenty of questions to practise adding decimals such as:

3.5 + 12.4   36.8 + 9.3   12.63 + 2.4   3.06 + 9.2   51.362 + 13.68   2.34 + 27.726

For a while this might interest some students who want to meet the challenge of trying to add decimal numbers. However, fluency often requires considerable practice and after 30 similar questions its unlikely that many students will feel motivated to do question 31! So one challenge as a teacher is to continue practice whilst still keeping students motivated and interested. One technique is to bring in a new topic such as perimeter, and continue the practice of adding decimals through the development of the new topic. For example, rather than have perimeters such as Figure 8, choose decimal perimeters as in Figure 9.

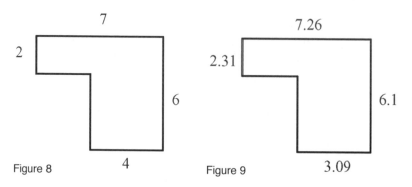

Figure 8

Figure 9

It can even be possible to begin practising a skill through subordinating that practice to a different topic which requires the same skill to be used (Hewitt, 1996). So consideration might be given to starting with the addition of decimals through work on perimeters, for example, rather than coming to perimeters with decimal numbers only after addition of decimals has been formally taught. Such an approach can give purpose to the learning of addition of decimals (see Coles and Brown, 2001 and Ainley *et al*, 2005 for some examples of trying to give purpose to work within algebra).

## In conclusion

Listening to learners is a privilege for someone interested in education. It is an opportunity for us to learn about our task as educators. But listening is not enough. For something to become significant involves bringing our own thoughts and interests to that event and to be prepared for those thoughts to be changed in some way through an encounter with a learner. Of course, we are all learners, not just children. So listening to learners involves listening to ourselves as well and allowing our thoughts to become more informed in the light of new encounters.

## References

Ainley, J, Bills, L and Wilson, K (2005) Purposeful task design and the emergence of transparency. In H. Chick and J. Vincent (Eds), *Proceedings of the 29th Conference of the International Group for the Psychology of Mathematics Education*, Vol. 2, Melbourne, University of Melbourne: PME p17-24

Coles, A and Brown, L (2001) Needing to use algebra. In C. Morgan and K. Jones (Eds), *Research in Mathematics Education: papers of the British Society for Research into Learning Mathematics*, Vol. 3, London: British Society for Research into Learning Mathematics, p23-36

Hewitt, D (1996) Mathematical Fluency: the Nature of Practice and the Role of Subordination. *For the Learning of Mathematics* 16(2) p28-35

Mason, J (2002) *Researching your own practice: the Discipline of Noticing*. London: RoutledgeFalmer

Watson, A (2006) *Raising achievement in secondary mathematics*. Maidenhead: Open University Press

# 2

# 'There are numbers in Australia': young children's perceptions of number and shape

*Nichola Abraham*

## Introduction

During my years teaching in a kindergarten I gained first-hand knowledge about the importance of mathematics in the early years. While working there, I did a lot of number work with children between three and four years old and was always amazed by the amount of knowledge they already possessed when they entered school. I found it fascinating how quickly children absorbed abstractions such as numbers and the amount of enthusiasm they showed when learning about them. When I had the opportunity to carry out two small research projects, I decided to investigate children's understanding of number and shape. Findings from both projects are explored in this chapter.

## Perceptions of number
### Approaches to the number research

I based my main research project on finding out about young children's perspectives on and feelings towards number. I wanted to know where they see numbers in the world around them and whether they know how they learned them. Do children think that only their teachers teach them numbers in the classroom, a formal setting? Or do they think that other adults with mathematical ability teach them in informal settings such as at home?

I had to take many factors into account. For example, I needed a method that would elicit and portray their perspectives while taking their age into consideration. I decided to use a range of child-focused methods to gather data (Rogers and Evans, 2008, p42). Young children may not always be able to communicate their ideas in ways that adults appreciate or understand. So I needed to find creative methods that would sustain their interest and would not require them to communicate only by writing or speaking. I wanted them to have the freedom to explore and express their own ideas, opinions and feelings.

I divided my method into two parts. I drew on research by Dunphy (2006) concerning children's perspectives on mathematics and used similar methods and questions. I chose semi-structured interviews because the children were young; the interviews could be conducted in a less rigid format and be more like a conversation.

I also drew on the work of Roberts-Holmes (2005), who discusses creative listening to young children and outlines an approach which includes use of cameras and walking tours. These ideas build on the work of Clark and Moss (2001), who developed the Mosaic approach. This entails collecting data or evidence from the child and parent in many ways. The data is pieced together and analysed, hence the name Mosaic. Adopting elements of this approach, I asked the children to take pictures of where they see numbers with a digital camera. According to Clark and Moss, 'cameras offer young children the opportunity to produce a finished product in which they can take pride ... photographs can offer a powerful new language for young children' (Clark and Moss, 2001, p24).

The research was carried out with eight children from a London kindergarten. Their ages ranged from 3 years 10 months to 4 years 2 months. The interviews were tape recorded and notes were also kept. To analyse the results, I looked at the questions from the semi-structured interview under various themes. These themes are explored in the sections that follow.

## The personal beliefs and feelings children held about numbers

One theme emerging from the interviews was the way in which children related to numbers personally. From looking around the classroom, I saw that a large section of it was dedicated to a birthday calendar. Each child's birthday was clearly written on a birthday cake and showed how old they were at present. This could be one reason why all the children were able to answer my question about how old they were. Four children answered this question without additional comment, simply stating 'I am 3' or 'I am 4'. The other four made additional comments, as shown below:

I am a big boy! I am 4! (Robert)
I am 4 and a half (Thomas)
I am big! I am 3 and a half (Teresa)
I am 3 and my little brother is 2 and my teacher is 11 (Justin)

The answers made me ask myself further questions. Did the children actually understand the concept that how old you are means the number of years you have been alive? Or have they learnt through repetition that this is the correct answer when asked this specific question? Both Thomas and Teresa added the word half to their age in years to represent that they are a little bit older. However, Thomas is 4 years and 2 months old, and Teresa is 3 years and 10 months old. Therefore, I am not sure if they are aware of what half actually represents. I also do not think that the children are fully aware of the meaning of years old.

Another interesting fact was that Justin stated that his teacher was 11 years old. Justin must believe that 11 is a big number, and because his teacher is big she must be 11. This comment was similar to those recorded by Dave Hewitt in the chapter discussing comments made by his daughters at a similar age. Dave suggests that the focus is first on learning number names and then on learning the relative values associated with them. When Justin was asked to count as part of the interviews, he counted unaided to 11, needed prompting at 12 and then counted to fifteen. This suggests that he is still learning names for the teen numbers and that understanding their value and knowledge of higher numbers will come later. Events earlier in the day suggest another possible explanation for Justin's answer. Before the interviews I sat in the class and observed the teacher talking to the children about the day, the date and the weather. The date was the 11th of the month and it was placed on the calendar by one of the children. When I interviewed Justin and he was talking about ages, he looked up at the calendar and said his teacher was 11. This incident matches an example given by Clark and Moss (2001, p18) where a child gives an answer prompted by a nearby object and this leads the authors to stress the importance of recording the context in which such discussions take place.

After discussing ages, I moved on to ask the children if they liked numbers. Two of the children said they did not and one gave a short reason.

> No, I don't like number (Thomas)
> No, because I am not very good at numbers (Teresa)

The reason given by Teresa for not liking numbers is interesting when compared with her counting. She counted the second highest of the eight children, counting to ten unaided and then, after prompting at ten, continuing unaided to twenty. She may have answered that she did not like numbers because of low self-esteem.

The other six children said that they did like numbers. Four simply answered yes, with no extra comments. The other two answers were:

> Yes, and I like to wear beautiful dresses (Chirsty)
> Yes, and I like drawing. And painting is the best thing to do (Robert)

A third question asked if they think numbers are important and why. Two children answered 'no' and did not elaborate. The other six answered 'yes' and gave reasons. One gave an answer which suggested she counted to conform to the expectations of others, a category identified by Munn (1997) in her research about pre-school children counting.

> Yes! When my mummy tells me they are (Teresa)

The other answers given were closer to Munn's category of counting in order to learn.

> Yes, because we have to count (Lucy)

> They show you what to do, they show you what to do with numbers (Chirsty)

Numbers are important. They can teach letters, how to count with. You write numbers and count numbers. When I count, they can teach you how to colour in and make sure you do not come out of the lines and they can teach you to draw better Rs for my name (Robert)

Yes. There are. Because a new school teaches me how to be numbers. It was Jeremy's, I just can't remember it. Because people come from places around the world (Johnathan)

None of the children mentioned counting to know how many there are, and this is in line with Munn's findings. However, one of the children who gave an extended answer also carried out actions while he was counting, as indicated below.

Yes, and letters, so we can squirt water out of the ranger. To help in to space and get to the moon. For running (he starts to run and counts to 10). For play dough, I mess it up (he puts play dough on the table and starts to count while he cleans it up) (Justin)

This fascinating answer can be interpreted in various ways. It has something in common with the findings of Griffiths (2007), who discovered that children counting at home with their families often counted actions. It may even indicate some early understandings of time, possibly as a result of hearing adults count either at tidy-up time or when they are in a hurry for some other reason. The reference to the moon could possibly be related to counting down.

## Social factors aiding children's learning

Teresa's comment above shows that discussion of personal views of numbers sometimes overlaps with the role of others. A further question that prompted answers of this type was 'Can you remember how you learned to count?' Through this question I was able to explore who or what children believe aided their learning of numbers. Their answers also enabled me to identify who helped this learning in both formal and informal learning environments.

One child, Teresa, suggested that no-one actually taught her and that she just knew numbers. This suggests that maybe Teresa does not completely understand that she was taught numbers at all. However, maybe she did not completely understand the question. Her answer was:

> No one, I just know! Sometimes I am good at numbers and sometimes I am
> not (Teresa)

Other children stated that it was their teacher who taught them to count
and one child explicitly said that it was only their teacher. This suggests
that these children do not see numbers as something outside the classroom which they can learn from others. They may believe that numbers
are an abstract concept and are only learned inside the classroom with
their teacher in a formal setting.

> Mrs Bianca, my teacher, and no one else (Lucy)
> Ms Maria and Mrs Bianca (Henry)
> Mrs Bianca (Justin)

Three children mentioned their teacher and other people in their lives
whom they perceived taught them to count. These children show that
they understand that numbers can be learned in an informal setting,
such as in the home. Finally, one suggested that a book helped him to
count.

> Mrs Bianca and Anthony, we do guitar lessons (Thomas)

> Mrs Bianca, I only have one teacher and lots of friends. At home, my nanny
> and my mummy teach me numbers (Chirsty)

> No! Mrs Bianca. And my friend Teresa teaches me to count numbers all the
> time and Lucy and Thomas. A lot of people, my teacher, my nanny, she is a
> new nanny, Clare, mummy, daddy, and my friends (Robert)

> I don't know! I have 'Eye-spy one fly' that I read at bed time. It has number in
> it and my mummy (Johnathan)

Another interesting point brought out, which follows the social theme,
was when I asked the children 'Can you count for me?' None of the children asked what objects they should count and just began to recite
numbers. Munn (1997) suggests that children believe that counting is
reciting a string of numbers in the correct order and that children do
not connect counting with quantification, which is the role it plays for
adults.

**Environments where children believed numbers existed**
Gifford (2005) argues that children learn through many factors, in a
holistic way. I was intrigued to see whether children suggested that they

learned through social, emotional, cognitive or physical environments. Depending on their answers, it would be possible to see which setting they believed they learned in and which settings promote their knowledge of numbers.

I asked the children where they can see and find numbers. All of them mentioned school, though only one child just gave examples from school. Justin talked about the birthday charts in the classroom and also pointed to a number line in the classroom when using the phrase 'on top'. Justin's answer is given first below, and is followed by the answers of three children who mentioned both home and school.

> On the calendar and on the birthday ones and on top (Justin)
> In my classroom and in my house and sometimes on the ceiling (Lucy)
> At the class. I do numbers at home and at school (Chirsty)
> In my bedroom at home. In the classroom on the wall (Henry)

The final four children gave extended answers implying an awareness of the bigger picture that numbers are all around. They are aware that numbers play an important role in their lives and are not simply an abstract concept.

> In my class, in a calendar, and there are numbers in Australia and that is a clock. And I have lots of rubbish truck and the old ones are broken (Thomas)

> On the board, and in my home I have timetables, in my friend's house. Numbers are everywhere (Teresa)

> We make numbers (He uses my pen to draw in my book). In the back corner, next door, in the school. I draw some numbers for you to see. And they are lots of numbers in shops (Robert)

> Everywhere! In my class. I have them at home and I will bring them tomorrow when it is show and tell. They might be numbers somewhere else, up there, (points to calendar) and in my work (Johnathan)

After the interview, the children walked around and took pictures of where they saw numbers in their school. Use of the camera brought a very positive result. All the children were able to use the camera and enjoyed doing so, which seemed to work as an incentive for them to find numbers in their environment. Use of the digital camera also allowed the children and me to have further discussions when we looked at the pictures they had taken.

Many children took pictures in the classroom: five children took photos of the number line and others photographed the calendar, number posters and number shirts. They also photographed objects including clocks, a calculator, a toy phone and a number book.

### Conclusions from the number work

The study's findings will help anyone interested in young children's mathematical development, including teachers, parents and carers. They show that children make connections between their maths class in school, and maths in their everyday environment.

My research agrees with Dunphy (2006), Gifford (2005) and others who say that children can and do learn numbers in both formal and informal settings. In addition, children can and do learn numbers from anyone and many things. The research also supports that of Munn (1997) which says that children do not understand why they count. Children's learning is aided when they understand the purpose of number activities such as counting.

### Identifying shapes
### Approaches to the shape research

According to current curriculum guidance for the foundation stage, by the time children have completed this stage at age 5 they should be able to 'use language such as circle or bigger to describe the shape and size of solids and flat shapes' (DCSF, 2008, p14). The purpose of this investigation was to see whether this target is set at a realistic level. I explored children's knowledge of the names of four basic shapes and was also interested to see if they could extend their knowledge and recognise these shapes in their everyday environments. I therefore asked children to take pictures of what they thought were shapes in their everyday environment and to discuss them.

Before I began the task, I spoke to the teachers about the children's knowledge of shapes and was informed that all the children had been introduced to and worked regularly with shapes. From my previous experience with young children, I knew that they enjoyed helping their teachers so I used games to present the task. I then explained to twelve children that we were going to play a game with shapes and that I was going to choose one child at a time to help me with the task. I took the child away from the group and asked them if they would walk around the classroom and find me a shape. When they found what they thought was a shape, they used a digital camera to take a picture of the object. Then, using the digital display, I asked them to explain what shape they thought the object was. To test their knowledge further, I asked why they thought the object was that shape. When setting the task, I gave the guideline that the children should choose an everyday object that had an obvious shape.

### Initial summary of findings

All twelve children were able to identify an object in their environment. Only one child, Alison, explained why the object was that shape. A further three children, Eva, Marilyn and Harry, correctly identified the name of a shape that clearly corresponded to the chosen object. These four children therefore clearly achieved the task's aim. All of the children's responses are shown in Table One.

Table 1: Children Identifying Shapes

| Name | Child's response | Task achieved? |
|------|------------------|----------------|
| Alison | She pointed to the classroom clock and said 'The clock! It is a circle. The clock is a circle shape because it is round!' Alison used her finger to draw a circle in the air. | Yes |
| Eva | She pointed to the pin board next to her and said 'That is a square, the board is a square.' | Yes |
| Marilyn | She walked over to the blue board and said 'It is a rectangle'. | Yes |
| Harry | He pointed to the big blue board in the front of the classroom and said 'This is a rectangle'. | Yes |
| Alexei | He walked around the room for a few minutes and pointed to the corner of a board, saying 'This is a triangle'. | Shape is named, need to consider whether name matches object. |

| Name | Child's response | Task achieved? |
|------|------------------|----------------|
| George | He said 'That painting I did has a triangle in it.' | Shape is named, need to consider whether name matches object. |
| Sylvia | She found a circular container and said 'This is a circle'. | Shape is named, need to consider whether name matches object. |
| José | He said 'A circle' and pointed to the inside of a builder's hat. | Shape is named, need to consider whether name matches object. |
| Claudia | She found a picture of herself in a photograph and said 'This is me in the picture.' When prompted, was able to identify the shape. | Shape not named initially, but named when prompted. |
| Lionel | He walked over to a photograph and said 'Picture'. | Shape not named. |
| Rakesh | He ran into the home corner and screamed 'This is a sheep that goes Baa!' | No shape named. Object is irregular. |
| Seth | He ran into the home corner and said 'That is the pond we painted'. | No shape named. Object is irregular. |

Three children did not achieve the task. Rakesh and Seth were both unable to identify an object that had a common shape. The objects chosen were an irregularly shaped pond and a plastic toy sheep. Possibly the reason that they could not complete the task was that English is not their first language. Both may have knowledge of shapes, but possibly did not understand the instructions and therefore were unable to perform the task correctly. Also, during Rakesh's turn, Seth followed us in to the home corner and saw Rakesh showing me a sheep as his object. So it is likely that when it was Seth's turn he mimicked Rakesh's actions and showed me an object of interest to him.

Lionel was also unable to complete the task. He was able to choose an object with a regular shape, a photograph, but he did not state the shape's correct name. It seems that he understood the instructions but might not fully grasp shapes and their corresponding names. This target may be slightly above his capabilities.

The initial findings indicate that four children completed the task correctly but three could not do so. The account of their actions confirms this, however, for the remaining five children, more analysis is needed.

## A closer look at findings

Claudia found a picture of herself and was therefore able to find an everyday object with a regular shape. However, she only said the name of the shape when I prompted her. Strictly speaking, she did not complete the task correctly. However, she did show an understanding of the task when assisted. The other four children to be considered further all identified an object and named a regular shape. The issue is whether they were correct in saying that the name matched the object. There are three difficulties. First is the degree of accuracy required, as most shapes in the environment do not absolutely match mathematical shapes. Second, there is the issue of matching 2D names with 3D objects. The third issue, the main one considered here, is what the children were paying attention to when naming the shape.

Initially, Jose showed me a builder's hat, an irregular 3D shape. However, he then turned it over, said it was a circle and used his finger to trace the rim on the inside of the hat, that was nearly a circle. He photographed the hat to show the inside. By his actions, Jose showed me that he understood. Alexei pointed to a rectangular board and told me it was a triangle, which was incorrect. But he photographed only the corner of the board and also placed the palm of his hand on the board to show me how the corner could be used to represent a triangle. He probably found it difficult to explain in words how he imagined the corner to be a triangle, but was able to demonstrate using his hands. Alexei's photograph also indicates a small coloured triangle in the corner of the board, which may have been drawn-on or may be the corner of an old piece of backing paper. Perhaps Alexei had noticed this. Close attention to the other two children's actions and photographs also suggests that they may be correct. Sylvia identified a container which had a circular rim and George's picture, although irregular and mounted on rectangular card, did contain some triangles on closer examination.

## Conclusions from the shape work

Looking at the initial results, only four children were definitely correct in their completion of the task. However, when investigated more thoroughly, a further five were able to demonstrate their understanding of how the mathematical shapes matched the shapes in the environment. On these interpretations, nine of the twelve children were successful. Therefore, I think that this early learning goal is set at the correct level for children in the foundation stage.

The investigation made me aware that assessment of young children can require more than just an instant judgement. My findings fit with the advice of Gifford (2005, p70), who suggests a range of effective strategies, including observation, indirect questioning and eliciting explanations to be used in assessment. All three contributed to my judgements in the shape task.

## Lessons about listening

In both of my projects, I was helped by using a combined technique which drew on the creative listening of Roberts-Holmes (2005) and the mosaic approach advocated by Clarke and Moss (2001). My findings in both projects suggest that we can learn a lot more from young children by combining approaches. In the number work children added to the information given in the interviews by pointing to things and carrying out actions. They also told me things when we were walking around the room and as a result of taking photographs. With the shape work, this additional information was crucial in informing my assessment. Like all the authors in this book, I advocate the importance of listening to children attentively. Also, especially with young children, it is important to interpret the word 'listening' widely to encourage children to demonstrate things to us with their actions and in any way they feel comfortable with.

My findings raised further questions. Did Rakesh mis-hear the instructions and think he was being asked to help me find a sheep rather than a shape? What was Justin trying to tell me with his demonstration of running and clearing up playdough? What part do numbers play in Thomas' guitar lessons? I was initially intrigued by Thomas' quote about Australia used in the title of this chapter. Was this an excellent way of showing just how widespread the use of numbers is, or was it a reference to something particular? Some time after the interviews, I spoke to Thomas' nanny and discovered that she was from Australia and was soon to return there. Our discussion confirmed that he made frequent mentions of Australia. This was a good example of piecing together information from both children and adults, as advocated by the mosaic approach.

I have learned a lot by exploring and analysing children's perspectives. The information I have gathered has broadened my knowledge and confidence about learning from children. I will take away many lessons from this study that will help me to become a better teacher.

## References

Clark, A and Moss,P (2001) *Listening to Young Children: The Mosaic Approach.* London: National Children's Bureau and Joseph Rowntree Foundation

Department for Children, Schools and Families (2008) *Early Years Foundation Stage: Statutory framework and guidance*, revised edition, Nottingham: DCSF Publications

Dunphy, E. (2006) The development of young children's number sense through participation in sociocultural activity: profiles of two children. *European Early Childhood Education Research Journal* 14(1)p57-76

Gifford, S (2005) *Teaching Mathematics 3-5: Developing Learning in the Foundation Stage.* Maidenhead: Open University Press

Griffiths, R (2007) Young Children counting at home. *Mathematics Teaching* 203 p 24-26

Munn, P (1997) Children's beliefs about counting. In I. Thompson (ed) *Teaching and Learning Early Number.* Buckingham: Open University Press

Roberts-Holmes, G (2005) *Doing your early years research project: A step-by-step guide.* London: Paul Chapman Publishing

Rogers, S and Evans, J (2008) *Inside Role-play in Early Childhood Education: Researching young children's perspectives.* Abingdon: Routledge

# 3

# Young children and adults listening and working mathematically together

*Hilary Evens*

## Introduction

This chapter shows how creating a listening and supportive atmosphere in a family numeracy project in an inner city infant school proved to be of value to the children and the adults working with them. Originally set up to support 4 to 6 year old children, who lacked confidence or were underachieving in mathematics, the project expanded to include parents who were not confident with their own mathematics but were keen to help their children and encourage them to take a more positive view of the subject. Three notable events are described in the life of a small group of young children and adults: a child who suddenly took initiative to the astonishment of the group, a session in which parents reported experiences of listening to their own children and a game in which children and adults listened to each other as they played and were led to try altering the rules.

## Listening to George

At the start of one session, a mother told us how pleased she was that her son George could now confidently count to ten. The news was received with delight by the other adult group members who were interested in all the children but took a special interest in George's progress. Aged 4 years 9 months, he was the youngest member and a shy, quiet boy who was receiving help from a speech therapist for a speech defect. We had all noticed that George's confidence was increasing, which his mother attributed to working regularly in this group.

On this particular day, the school hall was the only available space for our session so we used the games equipment for activities such as naming shapes, measuring and counting. As a finishing activity I threw all the beanbags into a pile in the middle of our circle of adults and children and asked everyone to estimate how many bags there were. We had often done estimating activities in previous sessions so the children and adults knew that they could not touch or try to count the bags but should make a guess and keep it silently in their heads until it was their turn to tell everyone their estimate. The usual procedure was that one of the children would then count the bags so we could work out whose estimate was the nearest.

On this occasion we were all surprised when George volunteered to do the counting, as he had never volunteered before. Indeed this was the first time he had spoken to the whole group and a few of us admitted later that we were rather nervous as there were clearly more than ten beanbags in the pile. George showed no nervousness as he quickly got on the floor and became totally engrossed in the task. He touched each beanbag in turn and counted out loud in his usual unclear speech that contained very few consonants, though we all understood what he meant:

'1, 2, 3, 4, 5, 6, 7, 8, 9, 10' and George shoved them to one side and continued:

'1, 2, 3, 4, 5, 6, 7, 8, 9, 10' and again these were pushed to one side

'1, 2, 3, 4, 5, 6, 26!' he shouted as he jumped up and went back to his place.

The other children, who had been carefully but silently checking his counting, were delighted and the whole group clapped. George's mother and the other adults were surprised and pleased by his successful counting and it was an excellent demonstration that children often know and understand more than we think. The incident gave the adults the chance to discuss George's specific achievement in our follow-up session and to link it with more general aspects of children learning number.

## What we learned from George

There is often more going on under the surface than is immediately visible. A particular opportunity can release what what may have been blocked or submerged by other social settings. Confidence in oneself and in members of a supportive group can allow a person to act in new ways.

In the incident with George, we realised that he now felt safe enough to count out loud and to speak in the presence of the rest of the group. We connected this with the supportive atmosphere built up by the group over the previous months, which enabled both children and adults to listen to George without interrupting, to pay attention to his actions and to notice that he could do more than anyone thought. The children seemed to have learned, perhaps implicitly, that they could follow George's counting despite his speech difficulties. They showed that they were sufficiently disciplined to support him quietly without interfering and then to enjoy his success.

It is possible that George's speech difficulty inhibited him from using the numbers after ten. He may have missed out eleven, twelve and the teen words because, in common with many young children, he found them difficult to remember. Instead, he found a way of doing and demonstrating the mathematics that got round any speech and vocabulary difficulties. Although George did not use the correct words when counting beyond ten, he showed that he understood the structure of counting in tens. He was also successful in matching objects to counting, even when the objects were in an irregular heap rather than in a line. So George's mother was right; he could count up to ten and, given the opportunity, he could count up to at least 26 objects successfully. Using his own unexpected method he showed that he knew that 26 was the same as two tens and a six. Previously, some of the parents had asked about the terms *place value* and *partitioning*, which they had seen on notices in the classrooms, so George's apparent grasp of these concepts provided an excellent example on which to base discussion.

It is sometimes assumed that children can count to 26 before they understand 26 as two sets of tens and six units. For George, things seem to have happened in a different order; he appears to have understood the idea of place value and used this to help him work out how many bean bags there were. This illustrates that children do not always learn concepts in the same order (Dowker, 2005). Perhaps the key thing to be learned from this episode is that George appeared to have at least one purpose for counting the beanbags. It was not a meaningless exercise. Perhaps he wanted to demonstrate that he could now easily count to ten, or wanted to find out how many beanbags were in the pile in order to find out whose estimate was the closest. Penny Munn's research (1997) on children's beliefs about counting shows that children usually start by thinking of counting as being a purely verbal activity and an end in itself, for example reciting numbers, 0, 1, 2, 3 .... It takes quite a long time for them to progress to counting with a purpose as George did.

## Implications and action

George's response to this activity has clear implications for formative assessment and planning. Sharing this information with others who work with George is likely both to please them and to present them with a challenge as far as planning for his mathematical development is concerned. The incident is also a reminder of the need to take a wide view of listening, as it was necessary to watch George's actions as well as listening to his rather indistinct speech, to understand how he was approaching the task. George's actions are also a reminder not to underestimate children who appear to have difficulties with mathematics: this issue is picked up again in a later chapter when Jenny Houssart listens to older children in bottom mathematics sets.

The activity also led to a discussion of different counting activities amongst the adults and what it was about this particular activity that motivated George. The discussion raised important pedagogical questions for the group:

■ When children are heard counting, how can you recognise the difference between chanting and actual counting?

■ How can you encourage children to progress from counting as recitation to counting for a purpose?

The answers to these questions are not always simple but being aware of them might enable you to look for opportunities to help move a child on from recitation to counting for a purpose. As a result of her research Munn identified four categories of counting:

■ Counting to please oneself, as a personal challenge

■ Counting to conform to others' expectations

■ Counting in order to learn the number names ie practice

■ Counting to know how many there are (adapted from Munn, 1997, p14)

These categories were considered by Nichola Abraham in an earlier chapter dealing with younger children: the issue of growing awareness of reasons for counting is also discussed in the chapter by Mary Briggs. Our chapters support the idea that as children get older they are more likely to understand possible uses of counting. The immediate issue considered by the family numeracy group was how to encourage children to progress in this way. The categories above can act as a reminder that activities like counting are often best driven by desire on the part of the learner rather than by a task imposed by the adult.

## Adults listening to children

George's revelation took place about a year after the group's formation, so a supportive atmosphere had been created and sustained. However, things were less straightforward and relaxed at the project's start. Parents and carers had joined the group for different reasons and with different expectations and were wary of each other in this mathematical setting. This required a supportive ethos for the sessions. We wanted to encourage the ideas of sharing, collaboration, questioning and listening in a non-judgemental and supportive atmosphere but this did not always work at first. For example, one mother, who had joined the group to push her son, boasted about his ability, much to the annoyance of the others. This needed tactful one to one discussions with the parents concerned.

Some adults found the sessions' informal nature different from their own experience of mathematics lessons when they were at school. Comments were made about these differences: they remarked on the emphasis on using equipment in their children's classroom and the use of correct mathematical terminology at an early age. They noticed that there were many opportunities for children to explain how they reached their answer and how the teacher listened, even if it was wrong. Most of them welcomed the new approach and recognised that the learning by the child was just as important as the teaching by the adult.

However Margaret, who brought two of her grandchildren to the sessions, found it more difficult to adjust to the focus on the child exploring and learning rather than the teacher telling the child. She could not bear to hear her grandchildren giving answers she thought were wrong and immediately corrected them, often telling them explicitly that they were wrong. This was a problem because I did not want to tell her how to work with her own grandchildren. So she and I worked together for some of the time as a foursome with the grandchildren and gradually she picked up the idea that gently asking appropriate questions could lead the children to note their own error and eventually reach the correct answer themselves. I soon noticed that she was aware of her hasty interruptions and was helping herself to solve this problem by covering her mouth with her hand as she listened. Some months later Margaret told me how much she had appreciated the sessions and felt that the elder of her two grandchildren had achieved a high level in the end of year assessment due to their joint participation.

Even before George gave his counting demonstration I was keen to emphasise that children do not necessarily learn things in the same order as each other and that we need to be aware of differences in learning. In preparing for the early sessions I had read Martin Hughes' (1986) work and was struck by the simple board-and-dice game he used successfully with 3 to 5 year olds. I made an even simpler one, shown in the diagram below, with two houses, A and B, and steps in between on sheets of A3 paper. Some of the families didn't own a dice so the group enjoyed making large dice from nets on A4 card. This resulted in informal discussion and sharing of information about topics such as measurement, accuracy and naming of 2D and 3D shapes. When it came to sticking on the dots one mother knew that the numbers on opposite faces of the dice add up to seven, a fact that surprised some of the others who had not known this.

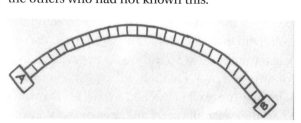

Figure 1. Drawing of the House to House game

Before taking copies home to try out with their children, the adults discussed the game. Vicky and Dianne were sceptical, thinking that it was far too simple to keep their children occupied. At the other extreme, Linda was worried that her daughter would not even be able to start the game. Immediately this was an example of differences in the parents' perceptions of how the children would tackle this activity.

Dianne was first to report back at the next session:

> Usually Damien [aged 6] doesn't like board games but he kept on wanting to play this one. As soon as we'd finished one game he wanted to play another. And he coloured the squares and made extra ones and made some short cuts. We had some fun making the rules and then changing them!

Dianne went on to say that she was surprised that Damien had wanted to play the game several times as she thought it was far too simple to interest him. Why would he want to keep on playing it? Other members of the group suggested that it was because Damien had decorated the board and helped to decide the rules of the game and make some changes, thus making it his own.

As expected, Linda reported that her daughter, Sophie, [aged 5] had found the game difficult but despite this, she was pleased with the outcome: 'She couldn't even make the first jump so I had to show her how to count starting at 0 and making the right number of jumps. But after a few goes she could do it'.

Vicky had given the House to House game sheet to her son Gregory [aged 6] while she made the tea:

> I thought he would colour it in but he didn't. He labelled the spaces 1 O 2 E 3 O 4 E 5 O 6 E 7 O 8 E 9 O etc. Then he said he'd made up two sets of rules. For the first game we had to use the numbers and for the second we had to use the Os, Odds, and Es, Evens. If the die landed on an even number go that many places, if an Odd, that many.

These rules created by a child and reported by his mother may seem ambiguous. Other members of the group did not question this aspect, but asked whether having two sets of labelled spaces meant that the game was over very quickly but Vicky said, 'no, it wasn't'. Despite her fears that Gregory would find the game too easy, he used the opportunity to be inventive and engaged in a task. His mother was able to listen to his explanations of the rules while she was preparing the meal.

Later group discussion enabled the adults to become more aware of the other children's grasp of mathematical concepts and gave them confidence to work with other children as well as their own. Parents also began to offer and ask for advice. For example, Mandy said that she would not let her daughter Annie [aged 6] do money transactions in a real shop as it would take too long and she would get embarrassed. Another mother said that she had felt the same way but had decided to go to the local shop at a quiet time and explain to the shopkeeper that she wanted her child to learn about handling money first-hand. Mandy didn't seem convinced by this but the next week she came in and told us that she had taken up this suggestion and reported on a successful shopping trip when Annie had used real money for the first time.

## What can we learn from this?

Based on their experience in the sessions, playing the House to House game with their children gave parents a chance to observe and listen to their child and in the process make informal assessments about their progress and needs. In reporting back sessions they were able to hear about the experiences of others and understand a little more about individual differences. Several commented that they liked the mathematics being made explicit in the sessions and welcomed suggestions from me as tutor and from other parents. Emily said she'd asked her husband why they hadn't been doing activities like this before. Another mother, earlier embarrassed by her own lack of formal mathematics said:

> Maths is easier to do everywhere and it can be fun – in the car, on the way to school, while cooking. In fact it's easier than reading to do anywhere!

The house game was clearly a popular experience with the group and confirms recent research suggesting that playing number board games at home can have a positive impact on children's mathematics (Ramani and Siegler, 2008).

## Implications and action

The groups' experiences in playing and discussing the house game have implications for choice of activities, adults' actions when playing games with their children and follow-up discussions.

The account illustrates the importance of the discussion following the use of the house game. As the group got to know each other and to relax, they became more open about sharing experiences and ideas. The story above about shopping is a good example of this. Recent advice advocates the involvement of parents in their children's mathematical education and also suggests knowledge exchange, where mathematical activities carried out as part of everyday life can be reported on in school settings (Williams, 2008). The discussions above appear to fit in with these recommendations. They also show parents' important role in starting group discussions and that the influence of these went beyond the weekly meetings.

The incidents in this chapter are all based on apparently simple activities with great mathematical potential. All of them can be simply understood and carried out with everyday or home-made materials. The activities can also be adapted by both children and adults, to make them easier or harder, to relate them to personal interests or ideas that have been recently introduced or to personalise them and indicate ownership. The selection of these activities was a factor in the success of the group and similar groups are also likely to benefit from a supply of simple but flexible activities with strong mathematical potential.

Playing games with young children can build their self-esteem through the attention they receive as they try out adult actions. This is enhanced if the adults are really listening to what the children are saying and doing rather than becoming irritated or trying to get the game finished. There are often opportunities for adults explicitly to justify their actions in a game and to invite younger players to do the same sometimes. In this way, children become used to thinking about their choices rather than simply reacting with whatever comes to mind initially.

## Adults and children listening to each other

Once an ethos of listening and respect was established between all parties, we were able to move on to games where children and adults could play on an equal footing. Rats, a variation of the game Race to 20, proved popular (Sharratt, 1999, p28). Instead of playing it with two people we adapted it so that the whole group could take part. Adults and children stood in a circle and at the end of each round the loser sat down when out. We then started another round and continued until there was one overall winner.

The first time we played, six children and seven adults were present. We stood in a circle, alternating children and adults, and counted round in ones from 1 – 20 for practice and to make sure the younger ones could manage, which they did with a little help from others. The rules were explained; we would take it in turns to count up from 1 to 20 round the circle with each person choosing to say one, two or three numbers. For example: the first person might say '1, 2', the second person '3, 4, 5', the next '6' and so on up to 20. The person who said '20' would be the winner of the round and the next person would say 'rats' and be out. This was a form of knock-out Rats as those remaining would then continue with another round until there was one person left, the winner.

We agreed that the first round would be a trial one, and the loser this time was one of the children, Amy, who promptly sat down with a smile. Her mother said later that she was pleased by this but also surprised because at home she usually lost with bad grace. We explained to Amy that it was only a trial round so she stood up and we started again. All the children seemed to be confident in counting to 20 though at first some had difficulty in choosing how many numbers to say. Jamie said four numbers and the other children gently pointed this out to him. By the third round, this problem had disappeared. By now the children and adults reeled off the early numbers but by about the number 14 the tension rose – who was going to be out?. They all watched and listened extremely carefully and those saying the numbers looked as though they were working out how many numbers to say so as to make it difficult for the next person. Some seemed to know they were doomed before we got to 20. Because it was played in a circle it was difficult for the adults to dominate so adults lost at the same rate as the children.

Only one child, Abby, made a fuss when she was out but she was ignored by the rest as they were keen to start the next round. The final two remaining at the end of this first series of games were Amy, the loser in the trial round and me and near the end I confess that I did deliberately try to lose so that she won. None of the children appeared to notice this but as we had already overrun our allotted time, they were hurried out for play time. This was the only occasion when an adult cheated to enable a child to win. In later games at least one child would have noticed if anyone was trying not to win and would have challenged that person. Children and adults alike really enjoyed this game and appeared not to tire of it. What surprised us all was that most of the children eliminated in the early rounds continued to listen to subsequent rounds and watched carefully to see what would happen, sometimes making suggestions as to how many numbers a person should say.

In later episodes of playing the game, children suggested variations. One child asked for a higher finishing number, another a lower one. Other changes included counting backwards, choosing up to two or up to four numbers at a time, instead of three. One of the 6 year olds had been learning about odd and even numbers in class and wanted us to use just even numbers. At different times we tried all the suggested variations and then the group evaluated them, usually agreeing that the original version was the best as many of the new ones were too slow or too fast.

Overall, the game gave excellent opportunities for listening, predicting and using strategies. It needed no equipment, could be played anywhere and some children took the idea home to play with other family members.

## What we learned from this game

Playing this game with young children showed the adults that young children can predict, devise strategies and adapt and vary conditions, often to a greater extent than might be expected. In general, playing games on an equal basis with young children can illustrate the many natural powers they possess and provide opportunities for extending them (Gattegno, 1981).

Playing Rats also provided opportunities for children to practise counting and for adults to check this. This game specifically requires children to start counting from a starting number other than one and to be aware of how many numbers they have counted. The ability to do this marks an important development and will assist children in developing efficient calculating strategies (Maclellan, 1997). Although Rats provided counting practice, it also presented children with a more difficult challenge of moving towards developing and perhaps even articulating, a winning strategy. This is consistent with the approach suggested by Hewitt (1996) who advocates subordinating routine practice tasks to more complex ones.

## Implication

Playing games provides an opportunity to discuss the difference between arbitrary and necessary rules, and the effect that changing the rules can have on the playing of the game. This provides valuable experience on which to build when rules of arithmetic are encountered.

Playing this game, with adults playing and learning alongside the children, gave the group the opportunity to consider the role of adults in supporting young children learning mathematics. The subject is considered by Gifford (2005) and four items from her suggested list, shown below, offered the group starting points for thinking about this:

- just being there as a supportive play partner
- being a conversationalist, negotiating meanings and speculating, 'I wonder why?'
- being a collaborative problem solver, modelling attitudes and strategies
- leading activities, but giving autonomy in choices and control (Adapted from Gifford, 2005, page 162)

The way the children reacted when playing Rats suggested that it was possible that at least one of them may have been developing an understanding of a winning strategy, either alongside or even in advance of some of the adults. This can be seen a unique opportunity for children to explain things to adults to aid adult understanding. Similar opportunities are discussed in Dave Hewitt's chapter and in the later chapter which explores what happens when children teach adults to count in different languages. An excellent reason for an adult to listen to a child is to learn some mathematics from them.

## Final discussion

This chapter has focused on children and adults doing mathematics together and listening to each other: child, parent, grandparent and family numeracy tutor in various combinations. Sue Gifford's (2005) consideration of young children learning mathematics shows that the role of adults is vital. She concludes that adult-led and child-initiated activities are both important for learning mathematics but that adult-initiated activities do not have to be adult directed. Adults can foster children's interest and enthusiasm for learning and create a safe risk-taking environment. They also have an important role in helping children to see what they are learning by providing language, focusing on feedback and fostering reasoning. Encouraging children to talk about what they have done helps them to be aware of their thinking, of how they counted or why they used a particular strategy.

One theme of this chapter has been intergenerational learning in mathematics. Less research seems to have been done on this than on literacy yet there is so much scope for mathematical activities in practical situations such as setting a table, or in leisure activities like games where an adult can listen to children. The family numeracy sessions helped adults become more aware of how they could be involved in the mathematics their children encounter and use. It is also important that grandparents, such as Margaret, can learn how to enjoy working mathematically with their grandchildren – if they see each other on a regular basis (Buchanan, Flouri *et al*, 2008).

The stories in the chapter show how adults can develop ways of listening to children that make shared mathematical activities more productive for the children. When playing the simple House to House game parents learned that being there as a supportive play partner and listener, rather than a teacher or leader, enabled their children to make choices and negotiate meanings and rules. Working this way in small groups gave children and adults more confidence in a larger group so that a shy child like George had the opportunity to demonstrate what he knew and children's suggestions for adaptations and changes could be explored in the Rats game.

It has not been possible to explore all the strategies used within the group. For example, the use of appropriate questions and prompts was vital in initiating discussions but has not been considered here as the focus has been on the children rather than on the tutor. Nevertheless, I have tried to outline some of the strategies which led to the success of the group. These included:

- providing activities which had strong mathematical potential but were simple in terms of outline and materials, for use in the sessions and at home

- establishing an atmosphere in which all participants listened to, respected each other's ideas and therefore actively shared them

- allowing time to reflect on activities, including those carried out in the session and at home.

## References

Buchanan, A, Flouri, E, Tan, J-P, Griggs, J and Attar-Achwartz, S (2008) Grandparenting: the growing influence of grandparents. *ChildRIGHT* 248, pp14-18

Dowker, A (2005) *Individual Differences in Arithmetic*. London: Psychology Press

Gattegno, C (1981) *Children and mathematics: A new appraisal. Mathematics Teaching*, 94, p5-7

Gifford, S (2005) *Teaching Mathematics 3-5*. Buckingham: Open University Press

Hewitt, D (1996) Mathematical fluency: the nature of practice and the role of subordination. *For the Learning of Mathematics* 16(2) pp28-35

Hughes, M (1986) *Children and Number*. Oxford: Blackwell

Maclellan, E (1997) The importance of counting. In I. Thompson (ed) *Teaching and Learning Early Number*. Buckingham: Open University Press

Munn, P (1997) Children's beliefs about counting. In I. Thompson (ed) *Teaching and Learning Early Number*. Buckingham: Open University Press

Ramani, G and Siegler, R (2008) Promoting broad and stable improvements in low-income children's numerical knowledge through playing number board games. *Child Development* 79(2) p375-394

Sharratt, N (1999) *Mouse Moves House*. London: Walker Books

Williams, P (2008) *Independent Review of Mathematics Teaching in Early Years Settings and Primary Schools: Final Report*. Nottingham: DCSF Publications

# 4
## Listening matters
### Mary Briggs

## Introduction

This chapter focuses on the value of asking questions of 5 to 7 year olds in Key Stage 1 in the UK and listening carefully to their responses so we can identify exactly what is happening and why. Do children really understand our instructions? How do they make sense of the tasks they are given? How does this help them to make sense of mathematics as an area of study? Why is it important to hear what children say and how as teachers do we ask useful questions? How can the teacher gain access to children's thinking even when they cannot hear all the discussion? In this chapter you are invited to try out some activities related to the issues raised here. These are designed to stimulate thinking about your practice or observed practice. They will allow you to engage with the ideas presented and hopefully give you food for further thought about listening to children.

## Background

This age group is an interesting phase of mathematics education for children as it heralds a change in the approach to teaching and learning in the UK. Previously children have been exploring with play and semi-structured activities in the Early Years Foundation Stage (0-5 year olds). When they reach Key Stage one there is a tendency to begin a much more formal approach to learning and teaching for mathematics. Children are taught as a whole class more of the time and even put into ability sets for mathematics in some schools. Effective teaching is seen as direct teaching which is teacher-led and dominated by teacher talk. As a result there is less time available to listen to children as they explore mathematical activities. This is when listening matters the most.

## The counters

Many activities within the 5-7 age range make use of counting as a starting point for the shift to calculation. The following examples come from interviewing children who have just started in year 1 and have been undertaking an activity involving counting. I was interested to explore with them what they thought they were doing and why. I used just three questions to explore this with small groups of children: How many things have we got on the table? Why do you count? Can you think of a time when you want to count things?

## Why do you count?

The following are extracts from the interviews with small groups of children using a box of objects for counting on the table in front of the children as a stimulus for our discussion, in response to the question 'How many things have we got on the table?'.

Thomas: Five.

Me: How did you know that? That was very quick, how did you know there were five?

John: 'Cos there was 1, 2, 3, 4, 5. (This was completed without pointing to each item in turn)

Me: You have counted them, but I didn't hear Thomas count them. How did you know there were five?

John: Why don't you put the yellow ones...

Me: John we're listening to Thomas as he is telling us how he knew how many there were on the table, did you count them as I put them out?

Thomas: Yes

Craig: I will count them first for you 1, 2, 3, 4, 5, 6, 7, 8, 9, 10.

Ashley: 1, 2, 3, 4, 5, 6, 7, 8, 9.

Me: Are you sure about that? We have two different numbers. Shall we count them together to find out?

All: 1, 2, 3, 4, 5, 6, 7, 8, 9.

I then asked 'Why do you count?'.

Kirsty: ummm

John: You know how many you have got.

Craig: 'Cos counting tells you how many you have got.

Lauren: It tells us to learn, it tells us to write our name.

Laura: To learn

Amy: To hear our voices

Kirsty: Because we have to.

John: You need to count because you have numbers.

Thomas: You need to count, as you need to know how much you have got.

Keaton: It's good

Sarah: It makes you so clever

Keaton: It's difficult

Lauren: If you have a friend that you share things with you can share things. Cos that's what my mum says, how you share things.

Laura: Cause your teacher's asked you to.

I followed this with 'Can you think of a time when you want to count things?'.

Craig: You could count how many hot wheels cars you have got and I've got loads of them.

Me: Right so you've got hot wheels cars and you'd like to know how many of those you've got

Craig: Yea

Me: Have you any idea how many you think you have got?

Craig: Yea

Me: How many do you think you've got?

Craig: I've got 71

Me: 71 gosh, that's a lot of hot wheels do you think?

Craig: Yes

Lauren: I count lots of things. I count stories, books, lots of things

## What can we learn from the counters?

One of the issues raised here is the kind of responses that research gains from children as they attempt to explore ideas as part of an interview:

> How can we trust what children tell us in research. We suggest that this is a question for all research participants, not just children ... In order to make some judgements about the nature of responses, we have found it important to be involved in on-going interactions within the research context and to build relationships that support this involvement. Knowing children, and their knowing the researcher, as well as the context, are essential parts of constructing meaning and interpreting the data. (Dockett and Perry, 2007, p51-2)

In my case I spent time in the classroom doing a range of different jobs so that the children and the teacher would see me as part of the classroom environment and therefore build up relationships with me as participants in the research. As a teacher you know the children and the context in which they are working in the classroom. The challenge for the teacher is to stand back from the situation and any preconceived notions they may have about individuals, based upon existing evidence. There is also the danger of the leading question, as can be seen with the first extract and Thomas. I asked him if he had counted the items as I took them out of the box but I didn't wait to allow him to tell me what he actually did. Waiting time is so important if we are to gain insight into children's thinking. This was a missed opportunity on my part but illustrates how easy it is for the adult to make assumptions rather than listening more carefully.

With the *Why do we count?* question you can see that there are a range of responses, with some perhaps not understanding the question asked and guessing what I wanted to know. The girls in this extract appear to be counting obediently because someone else tells them to rather than seeing a specific benefit to themselves as a result of the counting activity. Although the children in this chapter are older, this links to the findings of Nichola Abraham in chapter two where children are relating numbers to their age, making the numbers personal in their attempts to make sense of the mathematics. The children in this chapter can be seen to have developed some strategies to complete what is expected but still haven't fully developed their understanding of why they are doing the things they are asked to do.

In 2008, the Every child counts programme starts a roll-out to ensure that every child can count by the age of seven. The aim is to enable the lowest attaining children to make greater progress towards expected levels of attainment in mathematics and to achieve level 2 or where possible level 2B or better by the end of Key Stage 1 when children are either 6 or 7, depending upon when their birthday falls in the year. The levels are those expected against the National Curriculum for England in mathematics. So for teachers there is a current reason for looking at counting. The other issue is the basis on which teachers make decisions about children's understanding of topics such as counting. The children quoted above were all in one class.

What was interesting about these extracts from an interviewer/observer's perspective was the different judgements made about the children by their class teacher. Laura, for example, was seen as a good counter as she could recite the numbers in the correct order from 1-100 but when asked about why she counted she seemed to have no idea, except that her teacher asked her to count. In comparison Craig had a clear articulation of why he was counting and that cardinal numbers would give him a total for any set of items counted. In the classroom he was not seen as having any ability in mathematics as he could not recite the pattern of numbers correctly. Laura seems to count without any apparent understanding of why. For her it is a rote activity, completed whenever asked. Her approach could be characterised as largely instrumental, whereas Craig displays more of a relational understanding, since he has an understanding of why he might count but doesn't appear to have yet mastered some of the procedures involved as yet (Skemp, 1976).

## Do they understand why?
Choose two children in your class one who you currently think has some understanding and knowledge of a specific topic and one who you think may not have the same knowledge. Arrange to talk to these two children individually about the topic either that you have been working on with the class or perhaps a discussion about a new topic so you can hear about what the children already know. Try to think about what kinds of responses you are expecting and why before you listen to the children.

## Comment

The process of choosing children to talk to has hopefully set you thinking about how you make judgements about children's knowledge and understanding. You will have learnt about your own questioning skills trying this task as well as perhaps thinking differently about how children display their knowledge in the classroom and how sometimes they do not openly share their knowledge in this situation. The balance between instrumental and relational understanding we expect of children is a crucial question to ask when we are listening to children's responses and making judgements about them as a result of this information.

## Capacity Issues

The issues raised in this section come from an observation of a teacher teaching a whole class lesson on capacity with a class towards the end of year 1, so most of the children were 6 but some were still 5 years old. This was the second lesson in a series for this topic. The lesson started with the whole class on the carpet with the teacher. The teacher reminded the class that earlier in the week they had compared the size of different cartons by measuring how many cupfuls of sand it took to fill each container. The initial activity was a challenge to the class, 'Who thinks they might be able to beat me in a game of estimation?' The person with the closest estimate to the actual measurement will win £1. A boy was chosen and came out to sit at the front of the class with the teacher. She then showed the class two containers, one large tumbler and a smaller cup. How many cupfuls will fill the tumbler?

The boy thought this would be an easy task as the cup was quite big in comparison to the tumbler and so there would be only a few cupfuls to fill the tumbler. However at this point she also produced another smaller cup and explained to the boy that the larger cup was hers and the smaller one was his. Now there were cries of 'That's not fair!' from both the boy sitting at the front and other members of the class. They could clearly see that the teacher had set the task up so that she would win. The teacher then went on to explore the problems of using non-standard measures and gaining agreement from the children that not all cups were the same. The next part of the lesson moved on to measuring liquids and the teacher produced a water bottle and asked the question, 'What could we use to measure how much is in the container?' She had prepared some coloured water in a measuring jug and asked one of the class to read the scale on the side of the jug. The jug held a litre of coloured water and the teacher explained that a litre was a standard measure for liquids. The class were then invited to look at a range of containers that could all hold a litre of liquid. The main task for the groups was then explained. On each table the children had a range of containers and they had to sort the containers into less than a litre, about a litre and more than a litre. There were five groups of children, two of which had adults to support the discussion and the task. One adult was the teacher and the other a teaching assistant. The other groups were expected to work independently.

The groups who were working independently quickly completed the task, though there was limited discussion. What tended to happen was that the children moved the containers between the labelled sorting rings on the table, without reference to other members of the group. The teacher then realised that the children had finished and drew them together around one of the small tables to look at what this group had done. She brought with her the jug containing a litre of coloured water. She then took each of the containers in turn and asked the class if they agreed where the container had been placed, either less than a litre, about a litre or more than a litre. In order to check each one she poured the litre of coloured water from the jug into each container in turn. The responses to this part of the lesson were quite varied. Some children were easily able to identify which set the container should go into and why; others were not sure or were clearly influenced by their visual perception. When asked if they agreed with the decision made by the groups about their containers, the children's responses were partly based on friendships rather than an attempt to show their understanding.

When the teacher poured the coloured liquid into the containers there were some responses that showed that the children understood the categorisation of the containers. Others were clearly seeing things differently. When the teacher poured the liquid into a container that had a capacity greater than a litre and the liquid therefore did not fill the container, a number of the children thought that this meant that the container held less than a litre. They were looking at the space in the container that was not filled and mistaking more for less. Their attention may have been drawn to the empty portion of the containers. Some children in the class did not respond at all, so whilst it was clear that some of children had appropriate ideas about the capacity of the containers and that others were deceived by their visual perception, even more children gave no response at all so there was no way of telling what they thought.

## What can we learn from the account?

There are two different aspects to this short observational account:

1. Some children were clearly holding misconceptions about capacity of containers, based on their attention on the visual difference between the total capacity of the container and the volume that filled the container to one litre

2. In a whole class situation it is difficult if not impossible for the teacher to check that everyone understands accurately. Social influences and sense-based cues also inform behaviour, as well as the cognitive understanding.

## Perception deception

There are two parts to this task:

A: When teaching measures listen carefully to what children say about what they can see and how this influences their mathematical ideas.

B: Consider how you organise the class time to ensure that there is plenty of time to listen to children when they are working on practical tasks in mathematics. What do other groups do so that you can give your attention to a small group? How much time do you spend with the lowest ability group if the children are grouped by ability? Does the teaching assistant spend most of their time with this group?

*Comment*

A: The ideas of being deceived by visual perception is one you will be familiar with if you read about Piaget and his conservation experiments during your initial teacher training. There are other areas in measures where children see things differently e.g. when the balance goes up that object is the heavier one as it is higher than the other item, thus associating high and heavy.

B: This can be a challenge to ensure that most of your attention is with the group but the benefits are more accurate information on which to plan the next steps in learning for all children. This could include different ways of grouping the children based upon their responses, rather than using more global levels of attainment to put children together for mathematics.

## Asking about methods

Often as a teacher it is not possible to listen to children whilst they are working on tasks and so we pick up their written responses for marking. In this section we look at a small number of examples of children recording and what they said when asked to explain how they had reached the answers they had given. We will then look at implications for teaching and learning.

$$16+7= 86$$

'I thought I could just add the first numbers together' said the boy who had completed this calculation.

$$20+16= 35$$

The child said that she had actually counted on 20 more from 16 to get the answer.

$$78+65=1315$$

Here the child said that they added 7+8 to get 15 and 8+5 to get 13 and then wrote both answers down

$$14 - \square = 6$$

'This is what I did $14 - 4 = 10$ and then $10-4 = 6$ so the answer is 8.'

The child has combined the two 4s gained in trying to work out the answer.

## What can we learn from asking about methods?

We can make assessments about what children know or understand. We can identify errors, difficulties and misconceptions. Errors are simple mistakes that often children can spot and correct for themselves. Difficulties can be related to the nature of the task, instructions or affective domain issues, ie factors outside the classroom that have an impact on the child's learning. Misconceptions are fundamental misunderstandings about the mathematics presented. From all of these we as teachers can decide upon the next steps for the individual, group and class's learning. If questions are about work already completed, responses are less likely to be driven by trying to guess what is in the teacher's head. These are not closed questions but require children to elaborate on their written responses.

## How did you do that?

Look at any recording the children you teach have completed. Do you think you can see what they have done to complete the task? Arrange to ask a small number of children to talk you through what they have done. Try to choose work that was not completed too long ago.

### Comment

It is important that you try not to second guess the methods that children have used as this may affect the questions you try to ask if children get stuck trying to reconstruct their ways of working. There is the possibility that the child may be working in creative ways as a result of boredom with the task given and not as a result of underlying misconceptions about the mathematics.

## Gaining access to the dialogue in a busy classroom

Gaining access to all the dialogue in a busy classroom is a difficult logistical issue. What children say to each other is sometimes more revealing than discussions with an adult. Some of this discussion is likely to be about things, which are not mathematical. Checking out what they are expected to do may be part of their discussion, as is checking answers to problems or even methods used.

## Have you tried?

Find a tape recorder and place it on a table when children are working on tasks independently in a mathematics lesson. You will need to consider how you introduce the idea to children and to think about having it on a table long enough for children to get used to the idea of it being there to ignore it. So don't expect the results to be as effective initially as you might want but this is a technique that is worth persevering with for a while to gain the best results. Listen to the tape afterwards to pick up what the conversations have been about during the task. How much of their activity and conversation has been about the task? Can you pick up on dialogues about mathematical ideas?

## Comment

This will work best with tasks that have a practical basis. The following list about what makes a good activity might be helpful when deciding what task to set.

Does the intended task allow?

- access for all
- possibility for extension
- possibility for narrowing or simplifying
- enjoyment

Does it offer/present?

- a practical starting point
- stimuli and opportunities for mathematical discussion
- stimuli and opportunities and reasons for children to work and talk together
- reasons for children to record their ideas
- clarity of underlying mathematics
- opportunities for repetition without becoming meaningless -both for teachers and children (adapted from Briggs, 2000)

Combining this approach with the recording can help give you access to children's thinking as they work on tasks. It is important that the task is set up to give opportunities and reasons for discussion as part of its design.

## Other strategies

Another important and useful strategy is to give children time to think, so allowing for waiting time before filling the space is crucial. Before expecting children to speak to the whole class, it is helpful if they discuss the question first with talk partners or small groups. They can try out ideas and see if they make sense before going public. This strategy also allows the teacher and teaching assistant to listen closely to specific children's discussion points before ideas are shared in a whole class or group environment.

Alternatively the teacher can present a problem orally. Then, working in pairs or small groups the children can re-state the problem whilst their partner or others in the group listen and record the key elements of the problem and together they check that all the relevant information is included before trying to solve the problem. This method also enables the teacher and teaching assistant to check specific children's understanding, not just of the mathematics but of the instructions.

Developing the practice over time can extend the notion of a written record so that children can have an audio recorder to talk into, or even use a video recorder to express themselves. This can support the move to written records, as well as being used directly to show the class, the teacher, or even parents, if the children agree.

## Conclusions

The important message of this chapter is that in order to be able to listen to children, teachers need to do two things. First it is necessary to create a supportive environment to encourage children to talk so they can be heard; secondly it is crucial to ask appropriate questions to elicit children's ideas. The suggestions made earlier about designing the tasks given to children is part of this process, as is the organisation of the class so that adults can spend time with children listening to what they say. Part of creating the right environment is setting the expectation that children will be actively listened to during mathematics lessons rather than merely expected to answer questions.

Aubrey and Dahl (2005) review effective interview strategies to guide any adult interviewing children. They cite Wesson and Salmons' (2001) work, which examined interviews with five to eight year olds and found that drawing and re-enactment elicited a greater number of items of descriptive information than a verbal interview. Although their work focused on emotional events, for this age group aspects of school and learning mathematics can be emotionally laden activities. These ideas are linked to the clinical interview approach developed from Piagetian theory by Ginsburg (1981). This is a method of investigation where the adult, in this case the teacher, varies their questions according to the responses of the child being interviewed. The key issue is whether the interviewer has the ability to elicit the child's mathematical understanding, rather than leading the child to make statements as a response to their own interjections. Listening carefully is a crucial aspect of this approach and this includes being able to sit quietly so that the child's flow of thought is not interrupted. To return to the title of this chapter; listening matters.

## References

Aubrey, C and Dahl, S (2005) That child needs a good listening to: Reviewing effective interview strategies. *Journal of Education* (University of Kwazulu-Natal) 35 pp99-119

Briggs, M (2000) Feel free to be flexible. *Special Children* 125 supplement pp1-8

Dockett, S, Perry, B (2007) Trusting children's accounts in research. *Journal of Early Childhood Research* 5( 1) pp45-63

Ginsburg, H (1981) The clinical interview in psychological research on mathematical thinking: Aims, rationales and techniques. *For the Learning of Mathematics* 1( 3) pp4-11

Skemp, R (1976) Relation understanding and instrumental understanding. *Mathematics Teaching* 77 pp14-15

Wesson, M and Salmon, K (2001) Drawing and showing: helping children to report emotionally laden events. *Applied Cognitive Psychology* 15(3) pp301-320

# 5

# Unofficial talk in mathematics classrooms

*Jenny Houssart*

## Introduction

This chapter focuses on unofficial talk in mathematics classrooms. Incidents from four classrooms in two different schools are discussed: they all contain children who are considered to be low attainers in mathematics. The children are between 7 and 10 years old and all are in bottom sets due to a policy, recently gaining in popularity in English primary schools, which groups children of similar attainment together for mathematics. The majority of the children had special educational needs and the groups included children from a range of ethnic backgrounds, some with challenging behaviour and some who were poor attenders or moved frequently between schools. These children fell into the groups that are in danger of not being listened to, as discussed by Ravet (2007) and Billington and Pomerantz (2004).

## Types of talk in mathematics classrooms

Some other chapters in this book consider talk in mathematics classrooms. Andreas Kyriakides writes as a teacher-researcher who takes careful note of the language used in his classroom and exploits opportunities to encourage children to express mathematical ideas. A similar role is adopted by Hilary Evens in her family numeracy work. There are likely to be many mathematics classrooms where questioning is used in this way but there is a great variety of practice as far as language and mathematics are concerned. Discourse can be limited and follow pre-dictable patterns in some busy classrooms (Brissenden, 1998). Class-room talk can be dominated by instruction and explanation from the teacher (Bauersfeld, 1995) or can consist mainly of question-answer-evaluation sequences (Sinclair and Coulthard, 1975). These are not the only possibilities, however, and studies of the culture of mathematics classrooms suggest that pupils usually become familiar with the un-written rules controlling discourse in their classroom. Such rules are part of the customs and practices which develop in classrooms and are shared by the participants (Voigt, 1998; Cobb and Yackel, 1998). The idea of different classroom cultures stimulating different forms of mathematical discourse is explored by Richards (1991). He identifies four domains of discourse associated with different cultures, of which one is the school math culture, associated with the standard discourse of mathematics classrooms as just outlined. Richards also identifies an inquiry math culture, which he associates with mathematically literate adults.

The classrooms considered in this chapter all had unwritten rules about what was expected as far as talk in mathematics lessons was concerned. Usually there was considerable teacher direction and routines such as pupils putting up their hands and waiting for the teacher to give them permission to speak. Alongside this official teacher-directed talk there was unofficial talk in all the classrooms, not sanctioned by the teacher, but nevertheless about mathematics. I start by considering a group of boys who frequently made whispered comments.

## The Whisperers

The incidents in this section were recorded in a Year Five classroom (9-10 year olds). As researcher, I assumed a role similar to that of the class-room assistants who worked in the room. Sean, a boy who often sat beside me, made whispered comments about the mathematics going on. Some appeared to be aimed at me, though the majority were aimed at no one in particular and did not require a response. Three other boys in the class also made unsolicited comments about mathematics.

I refer to these boys as the Whisperers because of their tendency to make whispered comments. Analysis of these comments, gathered over a year, indicated that in common with other children the Whisperers sometimes commented on the work given and on occasion answered the teacher's questions in a whisper. On one occasion when work sheets were given out, Sean whispered 'Oh no, not easy work again'. Further analysis of their other comments revealed that there were three main categories: these are considered in more detail below. In many cases these comments were made as whispered asides and a response wasn't expected. On other occasions the comments were louder and represented a challenge to the official classroom discussion.

## The whisperers make discoveries

Some whispered comments suggested that the boys wished to share something they had noticed or discovered. In the example below, Wesley had apparently discovered how to use the constant function on a calculator to generate multiples of a number. This occurred after he had abandoned the official task, apparently because he had noticed something interesting.

> The teacher asked the children to do 101 − 79 using a calculator and then gave the correct answer. Wesley became interested in the incorrect answer obtained by the boy behind him who sometimes had difficulty with the calculator due to poor hand control. The teacher moved on to discuss the next task, but Wesley continued to press buttons on his calculator. At one point he appeared to copy down a number from the calculator on the back of a digit card.

> The teacher started to introduce the written task, which was to do a page of subtractions using a standard written method, then check the results using a calculator. The teacher admonished Wesley for turning round and talking to the boy behind him. Wesley said 'I was telling him something about maths' but the teacher did not reply. As the books were given out later, Wesley told me what he had been whispering about. He showed me that repeatedly pressing the equals symbol changes the answer. I asked what was happening and he explained by clearing the calculator, entering 3 and repeatedly pressing equals to generate the three times table. I asked, 'So can you do any table?' and he replied that you '...can do the twenty-four times table.'

In this incident, it appeared that Wesley was offering the teacher the opportunity to share his discovery by saying that he was 'telling him something about maths'. Perhaps Wesley felt his action was justifiable and could have contributed to the lesson. The teacher appeared more concerned about Wesley being off-task than about what he had to say mathematically. This incident and others like it suggest that the Whisperers had a different approach to mathematics from the teacher – an idea explored elsewhere (Houssart, 2001). A further example was a discovery made by Sean. In this case his comments appeared to be addressed to me.

> During work on hundred squares, Sean whispered to me, 'Miss, the six times table is all even.' In the plenary at the end of the lesson, the teacher asked about this but Sean did not answer – it was already lunchtime.

Sean appeared to want to verbalise his discovery, though there was no apparent desire to have it widely shared or discussed. Ironically, the teacher did wish to discuss the matter at the end of the lesson. It is not clear why Sean did not engage in the discussion – possibly he was no longer thinking about the mathematics because the lesson had overrun into lunchtime. This explanation is consistent with Sean's behaviour on other occasions.

## The Whisperers extend or supplement ideas

The Whisperers sometimes added something to what the teacher was saying or to an answer given by another child. This could simply involve moving on to the next question or part of the question, but sometimes they spoke about an apparent continuing pattern or predicted what would happen next. In the example below, Sean added to what the teacher said by linking the idea under discussion to something done in a previous session.

> The teacher was introducing the idea of converting metres to cm, though a previous session involved converting cm to mm. When the teacher said that 1 m is 100 cm, Sean whispered 'A hundred centimetres is a thousand milli-metres.' The teacher moved on to talking about a piece of string, which he said was just under a metre long. Sean said in a whisper, '999mm perhaps.'

As this example indicates, the Whisperers showed an interest in linking ideas generated in previous lessons. The teacher appeared reluctant to do this, apparently preferring to stick to the material planned for each lesson. This was also evident in the teacher's reluctance to move forward to ideas due to be introduced in the future. The teacher's view was not shared by the Whisperers, as shown in the incident below.

The teacher was talking about language and compared the word angle with rectangle. He noted that the word triangle has the same ending and a triangle also has angles. Pedro said 'It's got three.' The teacher said that they were '...not doing that today.'

Another characteristic of the Whisperers was their preference for mental arithmetic, whereas the teacher encouraged formal written methods. In the next incident, Darren seemed pleased with his method for subtracting 11 and wanted to share it.

The teacher was reading out answers to the mental arithmetic test. Darren wanted to explain how he had done one of the questions, which was '...from 26 take away 11'. The teacher seemed to ignore this for a while and continued to give answers. However, Darren persisted and was eventually allowed to explain how he had reached the answer. Darren said 'Take away 1, 25 are left. Take away 10, leaves 15.' The teacher moved on to the next question. Darren's comment was not used or praised.

In this case, an idea put forward by a Whisperer was acknowledged. However, it was not exploited by the teacher, who did not engage with it. This was probably the nearest the unofficial talk of the Whisperers came to the official classroom discourse. For a short time the two types of talk coexisted but did not merge.

## The Whisperers point to errors or things they do not like

The Whisperers sometimes made comments about mistakes made by other children, often prompted by children being asked to write or draw on the board or to give answers to completed work. Usually, the Whisperers merely pointed out errors and inaccuracies under their breath. Sometimes, they went beyond finding numerical errors and expressed views about what is important and correct in mathematics.

The teacher had written $1/2$ and $1/4$ on the board and was talking about which is bigger. He pointed out that although 4 is bigger than 2, $1/4$ isn't bigger than $1/2$. He speculated about why this is and a girl put her hand up and said 'Size doesn't matter.' Sean said in a whisper, 'Size *does* matter.'

The Whisperers also occasionally made comments disagreeing with the teacher. This was sometimes about checking answers but occasionally they took issue with him on more fundamental issues.

The teacher wrote a 5 on the board with a 9 underneath it and asked if it could be a take away. The teacher was leading to the point that it must be an addition because '...you can't take nine away from five.' Although no one disputed this openly, Sean did say in a whisper, 'You'd go below zero, it would have to be a minus.'

## What can we learn from the Whisperers?

These whispered comments offer many clues about these four boys' mathematical preferences. Along with other evidence gathered over the year, they suggest that they liked to extend ideas, make discoveries and take issue with ideas they disliked. They also had a preference for mental and non-standard methods, a dislike for formal written work and an enthusiasm for connecting ideas across mathematics. The teacher was experienced and had worked in mainstream and special schools. His teaching style was designed to keep things simple in order to encourage children who had difficulties. The result was that he tried to give clear and simple explanations, to repeat ideas frequently and only introduce harder ideas when he felt the children were ready. The unfortunate consequence was that the whispered comments were not highly valued in the classroom and perhaps this is why they were usually made in a whisper.

During my observations I gained other information about the Whisperers which is not evident from their whispered comments. A striking common feature was that all four boys made only modest mathematical progress over the year. They did not realise the potential shown in their comments and did not perform particularly well in formal written tasks, although they had more success with mental, oral or practical tasks. Though the teacher sometimes acknowledged their positive oral and mental performance, the Whisperers were never among those he discussed as possible high performers in the end-of-year test or as candidates for moving to a higher set. Moreover, all four whisperers were boys from relatively disadvantaged backgrounds. Two were African-Caribbean and two were White. At the time the study was carried out, concerns had been voiced about the performance of boys (Arnot *et al*, 1998) and African-Caribbean children in British schools (Commission on the Future of Multi-Ethnic Britain, 2000).

## Shouting out

In the two years following the incidents described above I researched in three other classrooms. In all of them I saw examples of children engaging in unsolicited talk with a mathematical focus. Some such comments were whispered, others were offered in a normal voice and occasionally comments were shouted out. Unlike the Whisperers, those shouting out clearly wanted their ideas to be heard and acted upon. In common with the Whisperers they occasionally disregarded the classroom's unwritten rules. An example was Penny, who was relatively new to the school and did not always behave in the way the teacher hoped. One of Penny's shouted comments is given below.

> The teacher was being positive. He called out the names of various children and asked them to stand up. He then announced that all these children would be given a star because they hadn't shouted out. 'I haven't shouted out!' Penny shouted out indignantly. 'You were shouting out,' the teacher explained patiently. Penny grudgingly conceded that this was the case, but added 'I was trying to help.'

Penny acknowledged that she shouted out in an attempt to give an explanation. My notes for that lesson confirm that she had made several unasked-for comments, which she often did. For example, when the teacher had used the word product, Penny remarked, 'Same as times.' Penny often acted as a kind of unofficial translator in the classroom, explaining the teacher's actions to the rest of the class or paraphrasing mathematical words and phrases. Penny's comments could loosely be described as an extension of ideas under discussion, similar to a category of whispers identified above. Shouted-out comments in the other two categories could also be identified. Children occasionally shouted out discoveries, apparently because they were sufficiently excited to either forget or ignore the classroom rules. A good example is Neil, who did not normally get excited about mathematics and appeared to find the subject very difficult.

> The teacher was holding up numbers and the children had to work out what had to be added to each number to make 20. She held up 14 and then prompted the children by saying 'What do you put with 4 to make 10?' 'I get it!' Neil shouted suddenly, getting very excited. Looking at his number fan, he said 'Mr Sixy, where are you?' In case anyone was in any doubt, this was followed by the comments, 'I know, I know!'

I also heard shouted-out comments in the final category of whispers, that is pointing to something they disagreed with or didn't like. Usually those making such comments were considered not to be averse to breaking classroom rules. There was one strong exception to this, where a girl called Lauren who normally cooperated with the teacher made a sudden intervention during the lesson.

> The teacher had drawn a rectangle on the board and then drew the diagonals. He explained that the sections of the rectangle were quarters. At this point, Lauren shouted out, 'How could that be quarters?' She stood up and went uninvited to the blackboard and continued her explanation, '...because that bit ', she said, touching the triangle formed by the longer side of the rectangle, 'is not equal to that bit.' At this point she touched the triangle formed by the shorter side of the rectangle. The teacher did not engage directly with the issue of whether or not the sections were equal, or the underlying issue of what equal means in this context. However, he did acknowledge Lauren's intervention by rubbing out the diagonals and dividing the rectangle into quarters using horizontal and vertical lines.

## What can we learn from Shouters?

The children who shouted out, like the Whisperers were engaging in mathematics. In Neil's case, his comment suggests that he had just fully understood an idea that the teacher had been working on for some time. This was useful information for the adults in the room, who were also pleased to learn that Neil was proud of making this discovery. Penny's comments, with her desire to help others in the class, also showed that she appeared to take learning mathematics seriously. Listening to her comments also gives an interesting indication of which parts of the teachers' explanation were considered to need additions. Finally, Lauren's comment showed her identifying a relatively complex mathematical idea in a routine lesson. We can learn something about mathematics and about these children's attitudes to mathematics in all three comments but we also receive a wider message about their desire to make sense of what is going on and to play a part in it. This contrasts with the view of shouting out held in some classrooms, implying that these children are disruptive and not interested in the lesson. Moreover, all these incidents occurred in bottom sets. It is often suggested that such sets contain many children exhibiting challenging behaviour and therefore teachers focus on establishing clear ground rules, for example by banning shouting out. My findings suggest that such a rule, though understandable, may not help all the children's mathematical learning.

## Opportunity or threat?

I have argued elsewhere that the Whisperers could be seen as representing a mathematical subculture with approaches to and views of mathematics which differ from those of the teacher (Houssart, 2001). It is harder to locate both the Whisperers and the Shouters in the wide literature concerning school and classroom cultures, derived mainly from ethnographic research in secondary schools. Willis' (1977) key work studied a group of young, non-academic, disaffected males who constituted the counter-school culture known as the Lads. The Whisperers do not share the open opposition to authority and to learning demonstrated by the Lads, though they appear, in a less extreme way, to have different views from the teacher about learning. The Shouters-Out certainly do not meet most definitions of a counter-culture, as they do not necessarily form groups but often act independently. Nevertheless, they demonstrate a deviation from expected classroom behaviour.

Ball's (1981) research is also relevant. Ball linked the formation of anti-school cultures in a comprehensive school to the system of grouping known as banding, which involved teaching pupils considered to have roughly similar attainment in the same classes. It was noted that pupils in different bands behaved differently. So did teachers, with those in band two classes spending time criticising or justifying authority rather than dealing with the content of lessons. The subcultures concept is further developed by Fuller (1984) who identifies a group of black girls in a comprehensive school as being pro-education and anti-school. A study by Sewell (1997) of black boys in a secondary school offers a range of categories, including Innovators, who accept the goals but not the means of schooling. The incidents recounted here suggest that Whisperers and Shouters are pro- the learning of mathematics. By some definitions, they could be seen as anti-school, though another interpretation would be that they are anti- the rules and conventions operating in their mathematics classrooms. They may simply be unaware of these conventions or have forgotten them on particular occasions. A further possible interpretation is that the school is anti this group of learners, as rules and conventions are being established that appear to hinder their learning.

The behaviour of the Whisperers and Shouters may not be intended to constitute a threat, though it is still possible that their behaviour, or similar behaviour in other classes, could be perceived by teachers as threatening. There are several reasons for this. Such behaviour may appear to be a threat to discipline, or a threat to the plan to introduce things one step at a time in ways that the whole class can follow or it may present a threat to the teachers' mathematical knowledge.

Another possible interpretation of this kind of behaviour is to see it as an opportunity. Most of the comments reported above offer opportunities for rich mathematical discussion. They also offer chances for assessing children's understanding which may contradict more formal assessments and hence raise important questions. Under current legislation schools and teachers are obliged to take children's opinions into consideration and to listen to their views. Is there not a moral obligation to listen to the mathematical comments made by students and to take them into account when planning lessons? If teachers have such an obligation, does it exist for all pupils or do pupils lose this right by breaking the classroom rules?

If unofficial talk constitutes an opportunity, then a first step might be for all adults working in classrooms to listen to unofficial talk. In particular, classroom assistants or other adults sitting with groups of children may hear such talk. It is also important that the classroom team should share the knowledge gained from this listening. The following categories are worth listening for:

- Children have noticed or discovered something
- Children wish to extend or supplement ideas
- Children have spotted something they disagree with or don't like
- A child is translating mathematical language to assist the rest of the class

Another possible message from the Whisperers and the Shouters is that children should have opportunities to make comments in mathematics lessons without feeling they are breaking the rules. This is the norm in many classrooms, though it is sometimes associated with particular parts of the mathematics lesson. Some suggestions for encouraging mathematical comments follow:

■ Allow opportunities for small group discussion, perhaps with an adult present

■ Pause before moving on to a new activity and explicitly invite comments, extensions or other examples

■ Use the plenary for children to share what they have noticed or discovered.

## A final thought

When listening to unofficial talk I became aware that it often contained surprises. The Whisperers and Shouters were a constant reminder that I should not underestimate children or make assumptions about their understanding, an idea which is developed elsewhere (Houssart, 2004). This last example illustrates this. The boy involved was in a small group of 7-9 year olds who were considered to have difficulties in mathematics. When I heard his comment, I wondered just how much he did understand, both about mathematics and about the way classrooms operate.

> Damian had come to the whiteboard to convert an amount of money from pounds to pence. After a few attempts, he arrived at the correct answer of 250. He did not write in the units and the teacher reminded him by saying 'Were they elephants?' Damian smiled and wrote p after the number on the board. The teacher smiled as well and said 'Good, now we all know what they are.' As Damian went back to his place on the mat, he added in a whisper 'Potatoes.'

## References

Arnot, M, Gray, J, James, M, Rudduck, J and Duveen, G (1998) *Recent Research on Gender and Educational Performance*. London: The Stationery Office

Ball, S (1981) *Beachside Comprehensive: A Case-Study of Secondary Schooling*. Cambridge: Cambridge University Press

Bauersfeld, H (1995) 'Language games' in the mathematics classroom: their function and their effects. In P. Cobb and H. Bauersfeld (eds) *The Emergence of Mathematical Meaning: Interaction in Classroom Cultures*. Hillsade, NJ: Lawrence Erlbaum and Associates

Billington, T and Pomerantz, M (eds) (2004) *Children at the Margins: Supporting Children, Supporting Schools*. Stoke on Trent: Trentham Books

Brissenden, T (1998) *Talking About Mathematics: Mathematical Discussions in Primary Classrooms*. Oxford: Basil Blackwell

Cobb, P and Yackel, E (1998) A constructivist perspective on the culture of the mathematics classroom. In F. Seeger, J. Voigt and U. Waschescio (eds) *The Culture of the Mathematics Classroom*. Cambridge: Cambridge University Press

Commission on the Future of Multi-ethnic Britain (2000) *The Future of Multi-Ethnic Britain: the Parekh report*. London: Runnymede Trust and Profile Books

Fuller, M (1984) Black girls in a London comprehensive school. In M. Hammersley and P. Woods (eds) *Life in School: the Sociology of Pupil Culture*. Milton Keynes: Open University Press

Houssart, J (2001) Rival classroom discourses and inquiry mathematics: 'The whisperers'. *For the Learning of Mathematics* 21 (3) pp2-8

Houssart, J (2004) *Low Attainers in Primary Mathematics*. London:RoutledgeFalmer

Ravet, J (2007) *Are we Listening? Making Sense of Classroom Behaviour with Pupils and Parents*. Stoke on Trent: Trentham Books

Richards, J (1991) Mathematical discussions. In E. Von Glaserfeld (ed) *Radical Constructivism in Mathematics Education*. Dordrecht: Kluwer Academic Publishers

Sewell, T (1997) *Black Masculinities and Schooling: How Black boys survive modern schooling*. Stoke on Trent: Trentham Books

Sinclair, J and Coulthard, M (1975) *Towards an Analysis of Discourse*. London: Oxford University Press

Voigt, J (1998) The culture of the mathematics classroom: negotiating the mathematical meaning of empirical phenomena. In F. Seeger, J. Voigt and U. Waschescio (eds) *The Culture of the Mathematics Classroom*. Cambridge: Cambridge University Press

Willis, P (1977) *Learning to Labour: How working class kids get working class jobs*. Aldershot: Gower

# 6

## Matchbox algebra

*Alan Graham and Roger Duke*

### Introduction

We have been working on developing an innovative way of teaching fundamental ideas about algebra. Many learners struggle to make a clear distinction between terms involving a variable such as $x$ and numbers. Our approach is based on using matchboxes to represent the unknown letter, $x$, and matches to represent numbers. We have created a software version of Matchbox Algebra in the form of a Java applet which is freely available (Duke and Graham website). In this chapter we set out some background ideas that influenced the design of the software and describe how we trialled it with learners aged 8 to 11 years. By listening to these learners' comments, we were able to see how the computer screen pictures might help them to form visual imagery that supported their grasp of the idea of a variable, as well as to gain confidence in using basic algebra skills.

We created the software application to help learners achieve these aims enjoyably and effectively. Using the applet, most learners could get an intuitive feel for the correct number of matches in a matchbox by starting with relatively easy problems. Learners can often correctly guess the answer to these easy problems but may not be able to articulate why they made that particular guess. The software aims to help the learner understand the underlying processes in these easy examples and then begin to apply these processes to more difficult examples. Starting from solving simple matchbox equations using common sense, learners are invited to develop strategies involving adding and subtracting from both sides of the equation , and later, multiplying and dividing. As a result they start to see these processes as developing naturally from their intuition, in harmony with it, rather than an arbitrary method imposed by the teacher. At some point it is appropriate for older learners to make the transition towards a formal pencil and paper method for solving simple equations: this is an option provided by the software.

## Background thinking

Before describing the Matchbox software and its use with learners in greater detail, this section explores some general background issues that informed our thinking. In particular, the following three ideas are explored, based on the work of Celia Hoyles, Jerome Bruner and Alan and Louise Graham: using ICT effectively, learning modes, and practical maths.

### Using ICT effectively

There is a basic dilemma for software designers when considering the needs of learners using ICT in the pursuit of mathematical understanding. Put crudely, much educational software falls into one of two categories. In the first the software drives the learners – for example, with a programmed learning package offering multi-choice responses. In the second, the learners drive the software, for example when the software comprises a tool like a spreadsheet that is in the user's control. We were anxious to avoid the first option but never intended to create a tool that users could use freely. The aim was rather to create a software environment for which the purposes or goals were clear, yet in which the learner was still able to exercise their judgement and some degree of control. This can be something of a difficult balance for the software designer. In Celia Hoyles's words:

> If we want to design investigative environments with computers that will challenge and motivate children mathematically, we need software where children have some freedom to express their own ideas, but constrained in ways so as to focus their attention on the mathematics. (Hoyles, 2004, p160)

She goes on to identify the following three conditions for enabling technology to change pupils' experience of mathematics (Hoyles, 2004 p161):

■  The users of the technology, both teachers and learners, must appreciate what they wish to accomplish and how the technology might help them

■  The technology itself must be carefully integrated into the curriculum and not simply added on to it

■  The focus of all the activity must be kept unswervingly on mathematical knowledge and not on the hardware or software.

Taking her first requirement, we were aware of the importance of learners being given clarity about the nature of the software and the purpose of the tasks. As discussed later, this condition was achieved in two respects. First, the applets closely mirrored the earlier tasks that they were asked to do with real matchboxes and matches. Secondly, in both cases – using real and virtual matchboxes – the goal of trying to work out how many matches there were in a box was transparent and obvious to the learners. Hoyles' second concern, that integrating ICT use into the curriculum is essential, was also taken on board: this is elaborated in the next section where the ideas of Jerome Bruner's learning modes are discussed. Finally, to accommodate Hoyles' third point, initial trials of the software mostly involved the teacher or researcher being in charge of the keyboard so that issues of hardware and software were kept in the background. In subsequent trials the learners were invited to control the software themselves. We found that the learners quickly mastered the software environment and their focus remained on the mathematics provided a short introduction was given by the teacher.

### Learning modes

As well as considerations by Hoyles and others concerning computer-based learning, we were also drawn to the ideas of educational psychologist, Jerome Bruner. Bruner identified three worlds within which learning might take place, which he termed the 'material', the 'imagined' and the 'symbolic'. Each world requires different sorts of representations and these encourage a corresponding set of three thinking and learning modes all of which Bruner believed to be valuable and mutually complementary. These he referred to as Enactive-Iconic-Symbolic or EIS for short. Expressed simply, these involved physically doing something (E), visualising (I) and using abstract symbols (S). He explained his framework in the following terms:

> Any domain of knowledge, or any problem within that domain of knowledge, can be presented in three ways: by a set of actions appropriate for achieving a certain result (enactive representation); by a set of summary images or graphics that stand for a concept without defining it fully (iconic representation); and by a set of symbolic or logical propositions drawn from a symbolic system that is governed by rules or laws for forming and transforming propositions (symbolic representation). (Bruner, 1966, p44)

In most cases we organised the learners' work according to this EIS framework. The learners started by handling real matchboxes and matches, which is an enactive phase. This was followed by the main iconic phase in which the learners used the software applets. Finally there was a short symbolic phase during which some of the learners moved on to modelling similar problems using conventional algebraic symbols. Bruner did not see these three modes of thinking as strictly developmental but our experience of working with our learners on this project suggested that it made sense to start with the E phase, then to move to the I phase and end on the S phase. The ultimate goal was to lead learners into the world of algebraic symbols, where they had both a secure grasp of what the symbolic notation meant and were able to manipulate symbols confidently to a purpose when required.

### Practical maths

A key feature of matchbox algebra is that it is practical in the sense that learners engage with the concepts in a hands-on way. The benefits of working practically had clearly been in the mind of one of the authors in work in fractions carried out with teacher Louise Graham in her primary classroom in Brighton. Working with different classes of pupils aged 9 and 10 over several years, they developed an approach to teaching fractions which they based on the children designing and making their own fraction pack. A key element was that the children were given the opportunity to decide for themselves how to make these fractional slices. Using cardboard circles, the pupils created in turn halves, thirds and quarters. Their teacher, Louise, reported that as a result of this work nearly every child in the project achieved what many of her former pupils had not: they had been able to form the concept of what a fraction actually meant. For example, they discovered for themselves that there were two halves, three thirds, four quarters, etc. in a whole and could also see and feel, physically, why one third was bigger than one quarter. Both teacher and researcher concluded from this work that it was not just the practical, hands-on nature of the tasks that made the difference but the fact that the learners had been set a clear and purposeful goal, the point of which they could understand. These pupils also benefited from having developed a strong visual image for a fraction which they were able to draw on in their subsequent work on using and calculating with fractions.

In summary the three key elements identified in the DIY fraction pack initiative that were drawn on in the design of Matchbox algebra were: practical work, purposefulness in the task and strong mental imagery (Graham and Graham, 2003).

## What is matchbox algebra?

Why is algebra hard? Two key obstacles stand in the way of learners' understanding of this unpopular topic. The first is getting to grips with the idea of a variable: what does $x$ really represent?. The second is that, when presented with an equation, many learners are unsure what the mathematical goal is: finding the value of $x$ that makes the algebraic statement true. A feature of matchbox algebra is that it deals in simple terms with these two difficulties. The variable $x$ is simply the as-yet-unknown number of matches currently in the box or boxes, while the aim of the exercise is to try to work out how many matches are in the box or boxes. For example, hold a matchbox in your hand, add three loose matches and tell them that you are holding eight matches in all. The game is to guess how many matches are in the box. here the answer is 5, and finding it is equivalent to solving $x + 3 = 8$.

Make the game harder by showing them two matchboxes with the same number of matches in each. Tell them that the contents of the two matchboxes plus 4 loose matches is 10 matches. How many matches are in each box? Here the answer is 3, which is equivalent to solving $2x + 4 = 10$.

We have observed that these understandings are simple to grasp by even young children. We were interested to investigate whether they would prove to be a solid foundation on which they could build a more formal, symbolic understanding of these ideas.

While real matchboxes and matches are an excellent starting point for teaching matchbox algebra, there are practical difficulties for the teacher in setting up multiple problems of this sort. First, it takes too long for the teacher to place the appropriate number of matches in each box out of sight of the learner every time a new question is posed. Second, experience of working with older learners – aged 11 or over – suggests that they may feel that working physically with manipulatives or mathematical aids is babyish. So with older learners it makes sense not to linger too long on the concrete version of the problem but to move fairly rapidly to the software version of Matchbox Algebra.

These are three of the research questions which were in our minds when designing and testing Matchbox Algebra:

■ Do learners find it easy to use matchbox algebra and are they able to solve equations when expressed in matchbox form?

■ Starting with the matchbox approach, can learners easily and successfully transfer to solving equations using conventional algebraic symbols? In particular, do learners subsequently draw on the visual metaphor of matchboxes and matches after they have made the shift to symbols?

■ To what extent do learners understand the overall aim of the exercise? Are they aware that the aim is to work out how many matches are in the boxes? Is this concept easier to grasp in matchbox form than when presented with an equation to solve, to work out what value of x makes the equation true?

Other questions to be investigated at a later date include the following:

■ When using the Matchbox applet, do learners really believe that these adjustments to the original equation achieved by adding or subtracting boxes and matches to and from each side of the equation leave the number of matches in the boxes unchanged? Note that this is different from saying that the original equation remains unchanged, which is clearly not the case. Some learners may be suspicious about the whole business of manipulating equations to make them simpler on the grounds that they are simply changing the problem to a simpler but different one.

■ If given freedom to tackle the problems in their own way, what intuitive approaches do they use and how do they describe and justify them? How and why do they think their choices of operations make the problem easier to solve?

■ How does the experience of using Matchbox algebra affect their understanding of the idea of a variable?

**The learners**
In this section we describe the experiences of a number of learners of various ages who kindly volunteered to work through the software with us. Although the software was tested in both primary and secondary school classrooms, the conversations included here took place in private homes. Gender-preserving pseudonyms have been used.

We tried it out with three Year 4 children: Jenny (8), Cora (9) and Opra (9). These girls came to the Matchbox session expressing differing levels of competence and confidence in maths. At one extreme, Cora stated from the outset that she was no good at maths and she probably would not be able to do whatever was asked of her. Jenny, the youngest, appeared calm and said that she was looking forward to the experiment. Her general understanding of maths was good and she showed a fairly high level of confidence in tackling the tasks. The interviewer knew in advance that Opra's grasp of mathematics was extremely high and her mother had remarked that she was excited about tackling something new and challenging.

**Jenny (8) and Cora (9)**
Jenny and Cora knew each other well as they attended the same class in school so we chose to interview them as a pair. Their tasks remained mostly within Level 1 questions where there are no negatives and only one occurrence of x in each task. For example, they were faced with questions such as $x + 8 = 12$, for which the Matchbox screen looked like this:

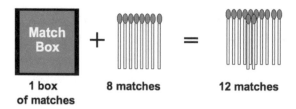

**1 box**       **8 matches**       **12 matches**
**of matches**

The younger of the two girls, Jenny, seemed more confident and capable of solving the problems. She was also aware that Cora lacked confidence in the task and on several occasions seemed to suppress her answer, looking instead to Cora to allow her the time and space to have a go.

Overall, Jenny answered the Level 1 questions fairly easily. When faced with the matchbox equivalent of $5 = x + 1$, she quickly answered '4'. When asked why she thought that was correct she replied, 'Because there's 1 add something and it equals 5'. At one point, a question was introduced involving more than one matchbox but with no negatives.

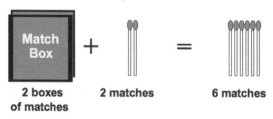

**2 boxes**       **2 matches**       **6 matches**
**of matches**

Sensibly, she tried tackling this by guess-and-check. However, at this point Cora started to object because she was being left out, so the idea of developing alternative strategies, such as sharing the matches between the two boxes, could not be pursued.

To help support Cora's understanding, the matchbox equation that faced her was presented in the following terms: she was told that the left hand side of the equals was the number of matches that Jenny had and the right hand side was the number that she had. She was reminded that she and Jenny had the same number of matches. For that to be true, how many matches did she think were in the box?

Based on this version of the matchbox problem, she was asked to tackle the matchbox equivalent of $x + 2 = 9$. She initially gave the answer 11, seemingly based on adding the matches on either side of the equals sign, which was a mistake she repeated several times later. At this point the interviewer felt that Cora needed a boost, so, without saying anything, he arranged nine matches in a line and then separated two off, as shown below.

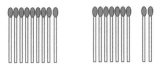

Cora watched this carefully and then counted out the larger of the two piles with seven matches. She then gave the correct answer, '7'. When asked why, she replied, 'Because if you take away 2 from each person and count how many are left'.

This seemed like a breakthrough for Cora, but sadly it proved to be her only real success. Cora needed much longer working at the enactive stage of the matchbox approach than Jenny, so the next fifteen minutes were spent modelling the problems using real matchboxes and matches. After a few false starts, Cora began to find it difficult to commit herself fully to the activity. Presumably because of her self-perception of low levels of success in mathematics, she did not appear to trust in her own ability to get the correct answer by using a logical method. Instead, she began to explore a range of highly creative alternative methods of deducing the number of matches in the box.

First, she had spotted that the interviewer had prepared, in advance, each matchbox with a particular number of matches in them and had written this number on a small piece of paper attached to the base of each box. While pretending to be concentrating on the mathematics, she quietly began lifting each box to enable her to read this number. Unfortunately for Cora, the interviewer's handwriting was so bad that she could not make out the numbers and so had to abandon this method. Next she tried gently shaking the boxes to gauge how many they contained – a more successful approach but by no means foolproof. Finally, when she thought the interviewer was not looking, she started carefully pushing the matchbox slightly open so that she could peep inside. The consequence of all these devious strategies was that Cora had, by now, totally lost any sense of how the answers might be calculated logically. The only positive conclusion from all this was that at least she had clarified that the purpose of the exercise was to guess the number of matches in the boxes, but she had not gained much else from the exercise. Like most learners with a low self-esteem and an unsuccessful history of learning, Cora had ceased to engage with the task as set and was actively seeking ways to create a different task that she thought she could do. By contrast, Jenny grasped the idea of developing a strategy and was starting to apply one with little prompting and with some success.

### Opra (9)

While Jenny and Cora were working with the software, Opra was feeling rather left out and kept popping over to see how they were getting on. As a result, when it came to her turn, she had a good idea of what Matchbox Algebra was all about. However, the interviewer felt that she deserved the treat of starting with real matches and boxes so he began to set out the component parts of the initial problem of $x + 8 = 12$, with unexpected and highly negative consequences. Opra immediately became highly distressed and backed off to the other side of the room, completely refusing to engage with the activity. It took some time to discover that she had recently had an unfortunate experience: her hair had caught fire from a lit candle. Opra had as a result developed a fear of matches so the interviewer decided to abandon the enactive phase of the exercise. In the event Opra picked up the ideas so quickly that this was never a problem.

When presented with the iconic matchbox equivalent of $x + 8 = 12$ using the software rather than actual boxes and matchers, she immediately said 4. When asked why, she paused before answering as if she was unsure what answer was required. She then replied, 'Because, round it up to 10 by adding 2, and 2 more to make it 12'. Being uncertain what the interviewer was really asking, she decided to answer why she knew that 8 was 4 less than 12. He was really trying to establish the nature of her understanding of what the matchbox task was about. However, she had such a sound grasp of this that she did not feel she needed to explain it.

Next Opra tackled the matchbox equivalent of $x + 5 = 17$. She quickly worked out that the answer must be 12 and gave as her reason, 'Because 17 take away 5 is 12'. Her attention was then shifted to Level 2 questions; these involved negatives. The first question was the matchbox equivalent of $4 = x - 6$. Initially she looked slightly puzzled and the interviewer needed to say to her that what this meant was, 'If you take away six matches from however many there are in the box, you're left with four'. She immediately worked out that there must be 10 in the box, 'because 6 add 4 is 10'.

From this point Opra decided that the interviewer was being too slow with the software and took command of the mouse herself. She had spotted how he had shifted levels and wanted to move on to more advanced questions. The next question she chose was the matchbox equivalent of $7x - 5 = 30$. Here she needed some help with a strategy. The interviewer suggested that to work out how many matches were in each box, it would be a good idea to get just one box on its own. She seemed comfortable with the idea that you could add positive matches to negative ones to get rid of the negatives, so she chose to add 5 matches to each side. This gave her the equation $7x = 35$. She then guessed the answer 5, which was confirmed when the on-screen box opened to reveal the five matches. At this point, the interviewer showed Opra the divide facility and she then divided by 7 to end up with one matchbox on one side and 5 matches on the other.

**Adam (11)**
Adam, eleven year old brother of Opra, shared her high level of confidence and competence in maths. He tackled just one question from each level, each of which he did easily. Soon he was facing the matchbox equivalent of $8x - 3 = 6x + 7$. Adam suggested that he should subtract 6 boxes from both sides. When asked why, he replied, 'Because 6 boxes is less than 8 boxes. You want to be left with boxes on one side so you subtract the smaller number of boxes.' This answer was pitched at a level of sophistication that the interviewer was not expecting from an 11 year old. The interviewer then translated some of the matchbox questions into algebraic form and Adam was asked to solve them algebraically, which he did fairly easily. It turned out that Adam had already done some algebra at home so this was not entirely new to him. After about twenty minutes, Adam was asked if the matchboxes had been helpful. He said that they were. When asked how, he thought for a few moments and then said, 'You've got the mystery box instead of $x$. It helps you ... to subconsciously know what you have to do. When doing the $x$ version of a question that you've just done with the Matchbox

algebra, it helps because I remember the steps I've just done with matchboxes'.

## The shift to symbols

A key feature of the design of the Matchbox Algebra applet is that it supports learners to make a shift from the concrete, or enactive, to use Bruner's terminology, to using mental imagery which corresponds to Bruner's iconic mode. Recent additions to the software have meant that it also supports the transition to the symbolic mode. For example, below on the left is the screen representing a simple matchbox algebra problem. Learners can decide for themselves what tools to use to tackle this problem: no tools, add and subtract only, or add, subtract and divide. But another option is open to them: they can at any time toggle the screen into symbolic form and use the same tool set to tackle the problem expressed in letters and numbers, rather than matchboxes and matches. This is shown below on the right.

In matchbox form                                    In symbols

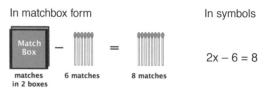

matches in 2 boxes    6 matches    8 matches

$2x - 6 = 8$

We have found that, when faced with the symbolic form, many learners get stuck and say, 'I don't know what to do'. At this point we invite them to switch to the matchbox form of the same question and see if this helps. More often than not they can see immediately how to proceed in which case they toggle the screen back to the algebraic form and proceed. What is encouraging for these learners is that the matchbox metaphor works in terms of providing a means of creating a strategy for themselves, rather than waiting to be told what to do.

## Discussion

Earlier in the chapter, three research questions were posed about the potential benefits of Matchbox Algebra. They have been paraphrased in simple terms below, along with some responses based on the evidence of listening to these learners.

*Did the learners find the matchbox approach to algebra useful?*
Evidence from these learners and others suggests that overall there was a positive response to the matchbox approach. With only one exception, Cora, they all found it easy to use the matchbox algebra software and were able to solve equations when expressed in matchbox form.

*Did it aid their use of symbols, particularly by supporting mental imagery?*
These are still early days with using the matchbox approach and the move to symbols was not pursued in depth for younger children. However, where it was pursued with Adam and Cora, confidence and interest appeared to increase.

*Did it support their grasp of the purposes of algebraic work?*
Although it is still too early to answer this fully, there was some evidence that the matchbox goal of guessing how many matches are in a box was a helpful point of reference for learners when it came to solving equations symbolically. Further investigations are ongoing.

*Other issues*
A number of other interesting general points also emerged from listening to these learners. First, the experience of working with Jenny and Cora as a pair emphasised the importance of interpersonal relationships within an interview situation. In this case there were three relationships to be managed: Jenny-interviewer, Cora-interviewer and Jenny-Cora, as compared with just one in all the other interviews. The interviewer thought that the Jenny-Cora relationship significantly affected the ways in which the tasks were chosen and tackled. In Cora's case, her fear of failure affected her capacity to think logically. It is also possible that Jenny's sensitivity to Cora's difficulties prevented her from fully engaging with the task herself which might have shown up Cora's problems and increases her discomfort.

Work with Adam was a reminder that when problem solving is examined in detail, chosen strategies are often more complex and subtle than they first appear. Many of these choices take place at an intuitive level and are never properly articulated, either by the teacher or the learner.

As with all software, there are many ways of using it: one teacher will stress one aspect and ignore others, while another teacher will emphasise something else. Although Matchbox Algebra may be played simply as a guessing game, it could be used in a different way. Here learners are asked whether they could manipulate each matchbox equation to end up with a single matchbox on one side and only un-boxed matches on the other. This emphasis might well encourage learners to concentrate on devising and practising strategies needed to solve equations, rather than applying a guess-and-test approach, with the simple goal of working out how many matches are in the box. This approach was tried in a secondary school – with some success.

## Conclusion

Although much of the listening to learners described in this chapter is based on one-to-one conversations between each learner and the interviewer, the matchbox algebra applets were actually designed for the classroom, with the interactive whiteboard as the preferred medium of presentation. This mode of use opens up many worthwhile listening opportunities for the learners. They may find that mathematical learning can be a shared experience where benefit is derived from listening to and learning from each other. Using applets in a group or whole class situation can help the teacher to stand back and listen to the learners talk through and explore ideas. As a consequence, this may help the teacher to identify those learners with conceptual difficulties, to better understand the nature of these difficulties and to start to devise strategies, based on the applets, to address them.

These and other issues to do with teaching with maths applets are explored more fully in Duke, Graham and Johnston-Wilder, 2009.

## References

Bruner, J (1966) *Towards a theory of instruction*. Cambridge, MA: Harvard University Press

Duke, R and Graham, A website www.mathsApplets.co.uk (accessed Sept 08)

Duke, R, Graham, A and Johnston-Wilder, S (2009) *Applets for the Teacher*. St. Albans, UK: Tarquin Publications

Graham, A and Graham, L (2003) DIY Fraction Pack. *Mathematics Teaching* 183 p16-18

Hoyles, C (2004) Steering between skills and creativity. In B. Allen and S. Johnston-Wilder (eds) *Mathematics Education: Exploring the culture of learning*. London: RoutledgeFalmer

# 7

## Learning to add fractions: a progression of experiences or an experience of the progression?

*Andreas O. Kyriakides*

### Introduction

This chapter provides an analytical account of listening closely to fifth graders (10-11 year olds) and tracking the learning trajectories of several students as they try to make sense of adding fractions.

The participants in my study were a group of 22 11 year old Cypriots (10 boys and 12 girls) whom I taught each day. Because I had to address all the objectives of fifth grade mathematics set by the curriculum of Cyprus, I could only teach addition of fractions once a week. The official medium of teaching, including the textbooks used and the tasks set in the class, was in the Modern Greek language. Though the instruction was almost entirely in Modern Greek, during class discussions and group work students spoke in a mixture of Modern Greek and Cypriot dialect. The mathematical terms used were consistently in Modern Greek because they came from the textbook which was written in the language.

Data collection spanned January to March. Being a native speaker of both Modern Greek and Cypriot dialect, as well as fluent in English, I relied on my own skills to translate the collected data. To secure validity and avoid any evidence of personal interpretation in translation I resorted to the process of Translation review by bilingual judges, which has been widely used in international comparative studies in mathematics. Applying this process to a sample of my data proved to be effective because 'in addition to checking the accuracy of the translations *per se*, it allowed checking cultural adaptations and comparison of the levels of reading difficulty' (Maxwell, 1996, p7-8).

Every week I reported my experience in a journal. My narratives included descriptions of classroom activity such as the tasks used and spontaneous dialogues with students, a summary of children's written work along with classification of commonalities and differences and personal interpretations of how the lesson flowed. The teachers' narratives along with original and translated students' writings and transcripts of audio-taped class discussions constitute the data for analysis.

The questions driving my research concerned the use of modelling activities in teaching addition of fractions and how these might influence my students' understanding; whether any shifts in students' thinking occur during modelling activities, and if so, under what circumstances these shifts in thinking occur.

The way I approached these issues is in line with Heyman's (1983) methodology in which the focus is 'on the interaction process whereby our sense of teaching and learning is created' (p23). The world of the classroom is perceived as an endlessly evolving process, 'as a world of becoming, a world which is created by our talk and action' (Heyman, 1983, p23). The heart of the classroom world lies in 'the intuitive sensitivity that can develop between teacher and learner and that occasions the deep learning that we all value and seek' (Mason, 2005, p472).

Knowing how difficult is to represent others' accounts of their lived experiences I will now step back and let my fifth graders talk. The teaching sessions I will describe here have been selected after 'zooming in' on and 'zooming out' of my weekly journal reports (Nemirovsky *et al*, 2005, p389). Zooming in enables me to focus on particular students, who spontaneously sparked insightful discussions and awakened my own and their classmates' awareness of the adding of fractions. Zooming out, on the other hand, allows me to transmit a sense of the whole by fastening together noteworthy incidents that arose at different times.

## What do learners say and what can be learned from listening to them?

I took the work on adding fractions as an opportunity to hold back and 'teach by listening', following closely what they said and did in response to the input stimuli which I gave them (Davis, 1996).

### Teaching Episode 1: 10 January

Jim, while working on the tasks $\frac{2}{10}+\frac{3}{5}=$ and said: 'These fractions do not have the same denominators; I don't know how to add them.' In the space provided besides the equal sign Jim wrote: 'I don't know.' In contrast with Jim, the majority of his classmates (16 and 15 out of 22, respectively) found the aforementioned sums by adding the numerators and the denominators of the given fractions.

### Teaching Episode 2: 2 February

19 out of the 22 students modelled successfully the addition fact $\frac{4}{10}+\frac{2}{10}$ but when the denominators changed into uncommon ones, $\frac{1}{5}+\frac{5}{10}$ the number of successful modellers declined to 7. Jim was among the successful modellers in both cases. However, prior to completion of the second task (see Figure 1) the following incident took place:

Jim rose from his seat and approached me.

Jim: How shall I do this? [He points to $\frac{1}{5}+\frac{5}{10}$] ... this is five ... and this is ten over here ... you see sir it's here where I always get stuck ... I don't know how to add when these [He points to the denominators] are different

T: Can you add oranges and lemons?

Jim: No.

T: So?

Jim: I have to make them the same... [He remains silent for a few seconds and then] This has to be ten ... two tenths ... ah, two tenths plus five tenths equals seven tenths.

Among the unsuccessful responses in the second task, Ria's is of note. She, as well as four other children, added the numerators of the two fractions to get the numerator of the sum and set number 10 as the denominator.

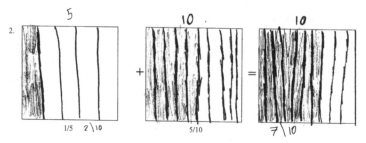

Figure 1: Jim's modelling of $\frac{1}{5} + \frac{5}{10}$

## Teaching Episode 3: 20 February

*Teaching Episode 3a:*

My pupils had so far been working extensively on developing their own strategies to add fractions, so I decided that it was time for a teaching intervention. However, I didn't want to expose them to a mere articulation of the procedural steps required. Rather, my intention was to orchestrate a learning environment that would inductively lead them to a conceptual understanding of why the change-into-common-denominators formula works. To achieve this, I employed technology-based representations in two consecutive 40-minute lessons. Before displaying anything on the whiteboard I gave out a worksheet containing three empty rectangular spaces and invited my pupils to model the addition fact $\frac{1}{3} + \frac{1}{4}$. Just a couple of seconds after I gave out the handouts, Jim got up from his seat and approached me, evidently puzzled.

Jim:     This [He points to the third rectangle] will be $^2/_7$, won't it?

T:     I don't know, think about it.

Jim:     But sir I don't know this ... I haven't known this [Adding up uncommon fractions] for long ...

jim had repeated this straightforward confession incessantly during the last few weeks but this time I felt that my intervention could not wait any longer. When the children gave in their worksheets I noticed that Jim, as well as Nikol and Ina, did not model the sum $\frac{1}{3} + \frac{1}{4}$ but only the two fractions (see Figure 2). Half his classmates added the numerators and the denominators whereas only one, Ramia, modelled successfully the sum of $\frac{1}{3}$ plus $\frac{1}{4}$. Among the other invented strategies Ria's stood out. Along with two other pupils she continued to set number 10 arbitrarily as the denominator of the sum (see Figure 3).

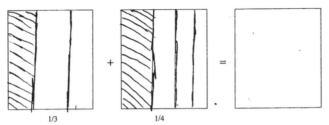

Figure 2: Jim's modelling of $\frac{1}{3} + \frac{1}{4}$

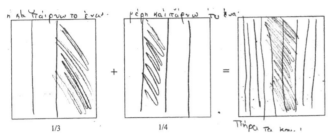

Figure 3: Ria's modelling of $\frac{1}{3} + \frac{1}{4}$

I chose to focus on Jim because his work showed that exposure to a series of examples does not in itself awaken learning. At the same time as the majority of his peers rush to extend the rules they had learned while adding integers Jim, in essence, repeats what Socrates stated in his Apology some thousand years ago: 'I know that I don't know'. This apparently deliberate resistance to compromising his ignorance of invented-substitutes such as, adding numerators and denominators, indicates to me that this 11 year old boy deserves to be guided rather than instructed so that he takes the lion's share in the construction of his knowledge.

*Teaching Episode 3b:*

T:      I set a task about $^1/_3$ plus $^1/_4$, who would like to share what they wrote?

Andy:  I found $^2/_7$.

T:      Could you tell us how did you find $^2/_7$?

Andy:  I divided the rectangle about $^1/_4$ into four equal vertical parts and I shaded one ... then I took the other rectangle about $^1/_3$ and I divided it into three equal vertical parts and I shaded one.

> In the end I added three and four and I found seven...then I added one and one and I found two ... $^2/_7$ ... So, I divided my third rectangle into seven equal vertical parts and I took the two.

Jim: But sir, I told you the same thing as Andy and you told me it was wrong.

T: Did I tell you it was wrong?

Jim: Hm ... you told me ... to think about it.

Nikol: I think that Andy's way is wrong because we cannot add a denominator three with a denominator four ... it must be ten, a hundred or a thousand.

T: Do you agree with what Nikol has just said?

Jim: I disagree because the ten, the hundred or the thousand is not related to what we are currently working on.

T: Who could tell me why we cannot add the three and the four?

Jim: Because they are two different things.

Just as every adult can experience mismatches between his own and others' interpretations and conjectures in a social group, so can children in their classroom environment (Doerr and Tripp, 1999). In Teaching Episode 3b, Jim seems to interpret the permission given to Andy to share something incorrect publicly, as an acknowledgement of the validity of his solution. Thus, he complains about the rejection of his previous question about whether it was acceptable to add numerators and denominators. Soon after, however, Jim regains his initial assurance that it is better to know that he does not know than claim that he knows something that in essence he does not (as Andy did for instance), and clearly expresses his disagreement with what Andy has said.

*Teaching Episode 3c:*

T: There were three kids; I think Nikol, Ina and Jim who did not write anything on the worksheet I gave out earlier.

Jim: I didn't understand it sir ... because I didn't know how to add the three and the four.

Nikol: The way I know is to make the denominators ten or a hundred or a thousand. Since four can be turned into a hundred and three cannot, I cannot make both the same.

Ramia: I know another way ... when the two numbers are consecutive we can multiply them ... and find twelve. Twelve is the smallest number in which both three and four get into. So, I made the $^1/_3$ four twelfths and the $^1/_4$ three twelfths. Then I added them.

T: Ramia's way is a correct one but I would like to hear how we can do this by using area models; $^1/_3$ plus $^1/_4$.

Ria: We take the first rectangle and divide it into three vertical equal parts and take one ... this is for $^1/_3$ ... then for $^1/_4$ we take the other rectangle and divide it into four equal vertical parts and take one of them. Then we take the third rectangle and divide it into ten equal parts.

T: Why ten?

Ria: [Pause]

T: What do the rest of you think? Do you agree with Ria?

Andy: I disagree because neither three nor four can get into ten.

Jim: I disagree with this way because three and four don't fit into ten so why divide my rectangle into ten columns or rows?

Xenios: I know why Ria said so because she didn't think before saying what she said that three and four do not fit into ten ... It was spontaneous...

Ria: It wasn't spontaneous...

T: This is absolutely fine Ria but if it wasn't spontaneous, could you tell us why you said ten? What did you think before saying so?

Ria: [Pause]

Jim: I know sir...she made ten because she used the area model to show it.

T: Okay, but why to divide it into ten and not into eleven for instance?

Jim:     Well, I don't know.

In Teaching Episode 3c we are witness to Ria's experience of an *impasse*. When Ria shared her own way of adding fractions she apparently felt quite satisfied; after all it was a strategy she invented for herself and had applied it in the past (Teaching Episodes 2 and 3a) without any authority figure labelling it as wrong. However, when Ria was confronted by opposition from her classmates she seemed stuck and preferred silence rather than arguing in favour of the correctness of her strategy. This signifies, as in the case of Andy, the absence of a well-established and confidently articulated basis for adding fractions.

*Teaching Episode 3d:*

T:       Now, I will show you something on the screen via the computer and ask you to look at this [Rectangular models of $1/3$ and $1/4$ are being displayed – See Appendix A]. How did the computer divide the rectangles?

Syria:   For the $1/3$ the rectangle is divided into three columns and there is one shaded. For the $1/4$ the rectangle is divided into four rows and there is one shaded.

T:       Let's see what happens next?

Jim:     It divided it into squares.

T:       Could you say something more?

Jim:     It made the squares and then it chose one column and it divided the other rectangle into squares and chose one row. In the second square the row has three squares whereas in the first square the column has four squares.

T:       Who else would like to say what they observed?

Xenios:  As the blue square [$1/3$] was three vertical lines, it took from the next one [$1/4$] which was four horizontal lines and it shifted from the red [$1/4$] to the blue [$1/3$] and as it was $1/3$ vertical it came the $1/4$ onto the $1/3$ and it became $4/12$.

T:       Yes, and what happened with $1/4$?

Xenios: As the red square was $^1/_4$ ... four horizontal lines and there was one chosen it took the $^1/_3$ which was three vertical lines and shifted it to the red one [$^1/_4$] and this became twelfths as well. But because the blue was divided into three and we shifted the blue [$^1/_3$] into the red one [$^1/_4$], we have $^3/_{12}$.

T: So we have?

Xenios: $^4/_{12}$ in the blue and $^3/_{12}$ in the red one.

T: So, can we find the sum now?

Ria: Yes.

Andy: $^7/_{12}$.

T: Could you tell us why is $^7/_{12}$ Andy?

Andy: Because we added 4 and 3, this is 7 and because both are twelfths we have $^7/_{12}$.

T: Now, could you tell us Andy why the way you told us in the beginning does not work?

Andy: Because we cannot add two different numbers ... it's like adding oranges and lemons.

T: So, we have to pay attention?

Xenios: The fractions have to have the same denominators.

T: Let's see how the computer will add the two fractions now that have the same denominators. What's going on here?

Ria: It took all the shaded squares and shifted them to $^1/_3$ and we have altogether seven squares.

T: So, could you tell us Ria what the sum is now?

Ria: $^7/_{12}$.

T: Would you like to tell us now why your earlier statement about making the denominator 10 is not correct?

Ria: Yes, because neither 3 nor 4 could fit into 10. As Ramia said before we have to make the denominator 12 and then add. $^1/_3$ is $^4/_{12}$ because we multiplied it by four and $^1/_4$ is $^3/_{12}$ because we multiplied it by 3.

Ria appears to refine her 10-denominator strategy as she experiences the technology-based representations in Teaching Episode 3d. The visual display of rectangular models, though quite important in provoking a conflict within Ria's internal representational system, would not have been successful unless the girl had also listened well so she could make sense of her peers' interactions. The last sentence of Teaching Episode 3d supports this and mentions Ramia's interpretation as a reference point for Ria's explanation. The value of this sentence lies in the fact that the last time Ramia spoke was during Teaching Episode 3c when Ria was mostly silent and apparently puzzled after acknowledging for the first time a mismatch between her own and her classmates' way of adding uncommon fractions. This analysis offers me strong evidence to assume that during Ria's silence multiple transitions in her thinking might have taken place.

*Teaching Episode 3e:*

Jim: I understood how it works but I am somehow puzzled with the movement of the columns and the rows ... how I will make it myself.

Xenios: You will not have to move anything ... just take your pencil and draw the columns over the rows and the rows on top of the columns.

T: Let's illustrate another example, $1/5$ plus $1/4$.

Jim: I'd like to say...

T: Do you get it now Jim?

Jim: I don't know ... the columns of the $1/5$ will be removed into the second square [$1/4$] and the rows of the other one [$1/4$] will go to the square of the $1/5$.

T: And now what can we do?

Jim: We can add them because...

T: Because what?

Xenios: The denominators will be the same.

T: How many squares will we have in each rectangle after the movement of the columns and rows?

Jim:     Nine...

T:       Nine what?

Jim:     Why don't you make it sir on the screen to help me?

T:       Nedi what do you think?

Nedi:    It will be 20 because 4 times 5 is 20.

T:       Let's see on the screen. Can we add now?

Jim:     Yes, because in the first square we have 20 and in the second we
         have 20 as well ... 4 in the first one and 5 in the second one make
         $^9/_{20}$.

The manifestation of technology-based stimuli is initially problematic
for Jim: 'I understood how it works but I am somehow puzzled with the
movement of the columns and the rows ... how I will make it myself'.
Xenios' prompt clarification sounds convincing to Jim: it refers only to
technical matters (eg how to reproduce the technology-manipulations
on paper). But is this Jim's major concern? In my view, the first part of
Jim's previous statement – 'I understood how it works'- indicates that
Jim is aware of the particularities of the example being displayed
(Mason, 2001, p48). This, however, does not satisfy him because it does
not provide him with the means to proceed independently – 'how I will
make it myself'. A few minutes later when I invited him to guess what
the denominator of the sum of $^1/_4 + ^1/_5$ would be, in terms of modelling,
Jim again requested assistance: 'Why don't you make it sir on the screen
to help me?' Though at that moment I did not pay much attention to
the incident, the more I think about it the more I recognise an innate
request from Jim to see the generality that would eventually free him
from the dependency on the technology-based models.

*Teaching Episode 3f:*

T:       Now, there is another way we can work when we have big
         denominators. Let's take an easy case first. For instance, if we
         have $^1/_3$ plus $^1/_4$, do you remember when we used to move the
         columns onto the rows and *vice versa*? Now, instead of moving
         them we will multiply both the numerator and the
         denominator of $^1/_3$ with four and both the numerator and the

denominator of $^1/_4$ with 3. And why do you think we do this manipulation?

Jim: Because we want to make the number below ... the number of small squares in each rectangle the same ... 12.

T: Well done. So, we will have...

Andy: 4 plus 3 equals $^7/_{12}$.

T: Let's say another example, $^1/_5$ plus $^3/_{10}$.

Jim: It's like drawing an X and multiplying one's denominator with the other two numbers and *vice versa*.

T: I would like you all to keep in mind the area models and how we shift the columns of the one area model to the rows of the other one and then *vice versa*. We will do the same here, it's just a different way of showing it.

Ramia: We will have $^{10}/_{50}$ plus $^{15}/_{50}$...

Jim: It is $^{25}/_{50}$ which is also one half.

T: Let's do another example, $^1/_6$ plus $^3/_9$, bring in mind the area models.

Jim: It is very easy now ... thank you sir in half an hour you made me understand it.

## Teaching Episode 4: 2 March

After the extensive discussion we had last week around addition of fractions via area models, I got the impression that many of my students understood the rationale underlying the change-into-common-denominators algorithm. To be confident I needed some additional evidence but would not collect it immediately after the discussion. Therefore, after an interval of ten days I gave my fifth graders the following scenario.

## Explaining to Anna

Anna found that $\frac{1}{3} + \frac{1}{4} = \frac{2}{7}$. When her teacher asked her to explain how she had worked this out, she said: 'Very easy, I just added the numerators (1+1) and found 2 and then I added the denominators (3+4) and found 7'.

If you were Anna's teacher what would you say to her?

The important thing is not only to tell Anna the correct answer but also to make her understand how we got it.

The scenario was not set up arbitrarily. It was chosen from the pool of responses my fifth graders provided me with during the last couple of weeks. Even though I intentionally omitted any reference to area models in the scenario, 14 out of the 22 students did successfully explain addition of uncommon fractions by drawing rectangular area models. Among the successful modellers was Jim.

Jim wrote:

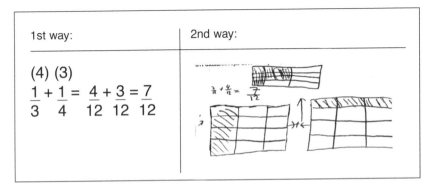

| 1st way: | 2nd way: |
|---|---|
| (4) (3) $$\frac{1}{3} + \frac{1}{4} = \frac{4}{12} + \frac{3}{12} = \frac{7}{12}$$ | |

Anna the way you did it is wrong and I would tell you why. What I did in both ways is to make the two fractions to have the same denominator because otherwise I cannot add them. In the first way imagine that I made an X, because the 3 went above the 1 and the 4 above the other and to find the denominator I did 3x4 which is 12. Then I did the 3x1 and I got $\frac{3}{12}$ and the other 1 I did it x4 and I got $\frac{4}{12}$. Now I can add them because they have the same denominator. In the second way I did exactly the same thing. I transferred the lines of the one area model into the other area model and the ones of the other area model to the other area model. These two ways Anna are the easiest!!!!

A key component of this analysis is Jim's interactive participation in Teaching Episodes 3d to 4, which reminds me that each learner has the right to experience the progression of their own learning. Jim's flexible responses reveal that he achieved the leap from the particularity of the illustrated examples to the general case of adding two fractions.

## What do we do with what we learn?

My intention in reporting these incidents was not to contribute to the extensive literature on children learning about adding fractions, but to show what holding back and listening to learners did for me.

I have used a single narrow focus in my attempt to hear what is not spoken and to see what is not displayed. Somehow in the process of sensitising my ears and eyes I began to refine past assumptions I might have had about the nature of learning the addition of fractions. The pedagogy of 'follow a series of examples and you will learn' does not sound convincing, because students may work on the ideas, detect the same and the different yet only follow rehearsed and laid out procedures step by step (Mason, 2001, p47). What counts, therefore, is not the reproduced but the novel arising unexpectedly in the world of the classroom. The current study indicates that the only way to enable learners to cope with the unconventional is to provide students with the tools to stir their awareness into the process of learning, into an experience of the succession (Mason, 2001, p48).

The rectangular area model suggests an example of a tool that might help the learner connect the known (part-whole interpretation of a fraction) with the unknown (find the sum of two fractions) and satisfaction in resolving it. Jim's publicly shared gratitude to his teacher (see Teaching Episode 3f) hints at this.

It would have been too sweeping, however, to claim that a medium alone generates fractional meaning. My classroom's observational data indicate that obstacles in progress, acknowledgment of mismatches between one's own and others' interpretations, incidents of questioning and conjecturing, along with effective use of computer software in mathematics instruction could transform learners' conforming practice. Instead of presumably ill-defined learning paths they would develop the confidence to reconstruct what they did and to innovate in future.

As Mason (2001) and Doerr and Tripp (1999) observe, teachers can help students experience the progression of their learning by provoking them to view their environment through a mathematical lens. This depends on the teacher establishing a classroom culture in which learners are ready to confront a broken expectation and in which they are eager to externalise their thoughts without being afraid to struggle publicly. But giving learners a voice is not one-directional; if we want our students to make the most of their learning potential we have to become sensitive ourselves: we must absorb and correctly interpret the classroom stimuli, spoken and unspoken, seen and unseen.

## Acknowledgements

This chapter is dedicated to my dearly missed sister and colleague *Georgia Kyriakidou* whose promisingly brilliant teaching career was tragically cut down by an automobile accident on January 16, 2005.

## References

Davis, B (1996) *Teaching Mathematics: Towards a sound alternative*. New York: Ablex

Doerr, H M and Tripp, J S (1999) Understanding how students develop mathematical models. *Mathematical thinking and learning* 1(3) pp231-254

Heyman, R D (1983) Clarifying meaning through classroom talk. *Curriculum Inquiry* 13(1) pp23-42

Mason, J (2001) Modelling modelling: Where is the centre of gravity of-for-when teaching modelling? In J. Matos, W. Blum, S. Houston and S. Carreira (eds) *Modelling and mathematics education: ICTMA 9 applications in science and technology*. Chichester: Horwood publishing

Mason, J (2005) Coming of age in mathematics education: 17 characters in search of a direction? A review of classics in mathematics education research. *Journal for Research in Mathematics Education* 36(5) pp467-473

Maxwell, B (1996) Translation and Cultural Adaptation of the Survey Instruments. In M. O. Martin and D. L. Kelly (eds) *Third International Mathematics and Science Study (TIMSS) Technical Report, Volume I: Design and Development*. Chestnut Hill: MA: Boston College

Nemirovsky, R, Dimattia, C, Ribeiro, B and Lara-Meloy, T (2005) Talking about teaching episodes. *Journal of mathematics teacher education* 8 p363-392

# Appendix A: Step by step display of adding up $\frac{1}{3} + \frac{1}{4}$ via the use of technology-based area models

STEP 1 $\qquad \dfrac{1}{3} + \dfrac{1}{4}$

1 third unit $\quad + \quad$ 1 fourth unit

CALCULATE

STEP 2 $\qquad \dfrac{1}{3} + \dfrac{1}{4}$

1 third unit $\quad + \quad$ 1 fourth unit

CONTINUE

STEP 3 $\qquad \dfrac{1}{3} + \dfrac{1}{4}$

1 third unit $\quad + \quad$ 1 fourth unit

4 twelfth units $\qquad$ 3 twelfth units

CONTINUE

STEP 4

$\dfrac{1}{3} + \dfrac{1}{4} \quad = \dfrac{7}{12}$

1 third unit + 1 fourth unit = 7 twelfth units

7 twelfth units $\qquad$ 0 twelfth units

CLEAR

# 8

## Can more be learned from interviews than from written answers?

*Hilary Evens and Jenny Houssart*

### Introduction

This chapter reports on research aimed at finding out as much as possible about children's mathematical thinking when working on certain mathematical problems and comparing what we learned from interviews with what we learned from written answers. We also wanted to know what children thought about explaining their answers in different ways.

The interviews came towards the end of a long-term research project about how 10 and 11 year olds respond to questions designed to offer potential for algebraic thinking. The project involved analysis of children's written answers to a range of questions. This gave us an interesting picture of how children answered many questions and what their difficulties appeared to be. During this process, we often felt that we might learn more by listening to the children talk about their answers than by analysing what they had written. So the project's final phase involved giving a short written test paper to children from three schools and following this up with interviews. The final page of the paper thanked the children for their help with the research, asked them which questions they found particularly easy or hard and to let us know by ticking statements, whether they preferred explaining in writing or by talking.

The children were interviewed in pairs and in the first part of the interviews were invited to talk about how they had answered the test questions. The major part of the interview was spent in tackling a question they had not seen before: this is reported elsewhere (Houssart and Evens, 2005). This chapter analyses spoken responses to a question which the children had already answered in writing.

## The question

This question is referred to as 'stickers'. It is a version of a sum and difference problem, a type of problem that has been around for centuries and is discussed, together with other related problems in chapter 10 of *Developing Thinking in Algebra* (Mason, Graham and Johnston-Wilder, 2005).

The version shown opposite was designed to be set in a context which we hoped would be familiar to most children of this age. The children were provided with a small box in which to put their answer and a large space where they were asked to explain how they worked it out.

Before we discuss the children's responses the reader should try this problem and make a note of the answer and how you reached it. You could also try to predict how 10 and 11 year olds with little or no formal algebraic experience might tackle it.

The interviews were carried out to probe more deeply the kinds of responses obtained from written answers in an earlier stage of the project when a sample of 364 children was taken from a range of schools. This provided some knowledge of how children might approach this question. The findings suggested that although most 10 and 11 year olds would attempt this question, only a minority were likely to arrive at the correct answer of 34. Of the many incorrect answers given, 38 was by far the most common with more children giving this answer than the correct one. For more details about how the 364 children responded to this question in writing see Evens and Houssart (2004).

## The Interviews

At the start of the project's interview stage, 10 and 11 year old children from three schools were given four questions to answer individually in writing under test conditions. A selection of the children were interviewed as soon as possible after the written papers, sometimes on the

Two girls have 60 stickers altogether.

Jenny has 8 more stickers than Hilary.

How many stickers does Jenny have?

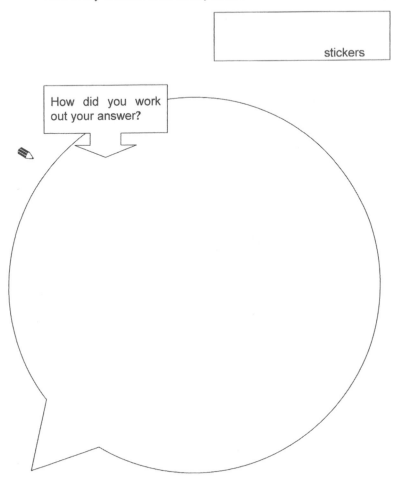

same day but always within two weeks. Nineteen interviews were carried out with 38 children who were interviewed in pairs. This arrangement was felt to be less threatening to the children and thus more acceptable to their parents and the school (Arksey and Knight, 1999). We also wanted to see whether the children would listen to or take notice of each other. Sometimes this happened and comments are included, where appropriate, in the stories that follow.

In preparation for the interviews the interviewer read through the written answers carefully and made notes but no markings or comments were put on the scripts and the interviewer tried to avoid telling children whether or not their answers or methods were correct. At the start of the interviews the children's written papers were given back to them and they were given the opportunity to make comments.

The stickers question was discussed in most of the interviews. One interview was unusual in that a child initiated the discussion rather than being invited to do so by the interviewer. In five interviews children commented on the stickers question when asked to comment on the paper in general and in three others the children waited until they were explicitly invited to comment. In three more interviews children started to respond to this question when they were asked to discuss their respective answers and in six interviews the children chose not to comment on the stickers question at all, sometimes choosing another question to discuss. One interview was different because a boy said that he found the stickers question hard but then proceeded to describe his feelings on written papers in general, as we can see later.

The following sections consider extracts from some interviews when the stickers question was discussed. They represent the difference in children's willingness to listen and take note of each other and to show the extent to which we learned more from listening to the children than from their written answers. One of the interviews also tells us about how one of the children feels about answering questions like these.

## Listening to Melissa and Leila

Melissa and Leila (all names are pseudonyms) were interviewed together, a pairing chosen by their teacher. In the written paper, Melissa had given the correct answer of 34, whereas Leila had given the answer 128. In her written work explaining her method, Melissa had used short mathematical sentences that indicated the steps in her reasoning:

$$60 - 8 = 52 \qquad 52 \div 2 = 26 \qquad 26 + 8 = 34 \qquad 26 + 34 = 60$$

Leila had supported her incorrect answer of 128 with the following written calculations:

$$60 + 60 = 120 + 8 = 128.$$

During the interview Melissa said she thought the sticker question was easy and explained how she did it.

> Melissa: ... I did 60 take away 8 cos I knew that Jenny has 8 more stickers than Hilary so I took away the 8 then I um got 52 and all I did then was I halved 52 to get 26 and then for Jenny's number cos she had 8 more than Hilary then added 8. 26 added to the 8 what got me 34 for my answer.

When the interviewer pointed out that she had gone further than this in her written answer, she said:

> Melissa: Yes. Cos then I were just making sure that all together [they] had 60 stickers so 26 added to 34 and I got the answer 60.

As Leila had not yet participated in this discussion the interviewer invited her to say what she did.

> Leila: I don't really know what I did, I can't remember.

When the interviewer asked Leila whether she had understood what Melissa had done, Leila replied that she had but did not seem to want to pursue her own method.

## What can we learn from Melissa and Leila?

Several issues emerge from the way these two girls talked about the question. Melissa was one of the most confident of those interviewed and never appeared to doubt that her answer was correct. Her explanation was given in a clear steady voice and matched her written answer. At this point the discussion was really between Melissa and the interviewer. Leila only spoke when specifically asked to do so. Even then her answer was brief and, far from adding to her written explanation, actually said less.

It is hard to interpret Leila's comments with certainty. One possibility is that she had a reason for her method at the time of writing it but had genuinely forgotten by the time she was interviewed. Another possibility is that she simply did something with the numbers in the written question and did not seriously believe that this was the correct method. A more likely reason is that, in the face of Melissa's confident explanation, she began to doubt her own method and decided not to expose her own thinking.

The interview does not add substantially to what we can tell about their answers from their written scripts, though it does suggest that Melissa was confident in her answer and method and Leila was, or became, less confident. Neither changed their answers as a result of the interview. This was true for all those who arrived at the correct answer during the written paper. Some who arrived at the wrong answer changed their answer during the interview but there were also several examples of children like Leila who did not offer to do so. The presence of an interview partner giving a correct answer and explanation did not encourage Leila to revise her own answer though it may have led her to doubt what she had written. A final important point is that the girls did not appear to engage with each other in this part of the interview whereas there was more dialogue when they tackled a new question later. On the later occasion Leila gave a more confident explanation before Melissa though Melissa was still the more assured speaker.

## Listening to Darren and Gregory

We had decided not to include any children in our research who, in their teachers' opinion, were likely to find the work difficult: this usually meant those considered to be working at Level 2 of the English national curriculum. However, one such child, Darren, slipped into the interview stage by accident. His teacher had paired him with Gregory and they were comfortable together. As he was keen to take part and permission had also been obtained from his parents, it seemed churlish to turn him away.

Gregory's final written answer was 34 but he had done two sets of working out. The first one, $^1/_2$ 60 = 30 + 8 38 + 22 = 60, was crossed out twice and replaced with: 34 + 26 difference of 8 6 + 4 = 10 30 + 20 = 50 10 + 50 = 60.

Darren's final answer to the stickers question was 12, possibly written over an initial answer of 28. He had drawn a number line with 60 on the left, 30 in the middle and 12 on the right with two jumps. When the interviewer asked the two boys whether they wanted to comment on anything on the written paper Darren immediately said:

> I found that one quite hard [*pointing to the stickers question*] because I didn't like understand it saying show how you working out and just ...

It is not surprising that Darren found this question hard but he seemed to welcome the opportunity to talk about how he approached the written paper and in his slow matter-of-fact way went on to say:

> I like read it a couple of times and then went on to the next one and then went back to it and I got ... and I thought a minute and then I thought of the methods we used er we've used in class the methods we've used in class

Gregory also said he found the stickers question hard and volunteered his explanation:

> Gregory: I found that number 3 harder than the others cos you need to like just have the number that you can guess at which has a number 8 and then you sort of get difference right [*pause*] between them {pause] to make 60.

Gregory then said that pictures can help you understand a question better which led Darren to expand on his previous comments:

> Yes and then if you don't have pictures on it when you get stuck it's like you don't know what to do and you just get like ... worried and then you start getting into a panic because you don't know what it is and then all you do is to turn over to the next page and then if you may like and then like once you've done that you keep going through them ones and then once you've done the rest you go back to it and then you see if you can try and do it and then if you can't you just hope you try your best and use your methods or if you don't have no idea at all ... then just do it . .

## What can we learn from Darren and Gregory?

Gregory responded to the interviews in a similar way to Melissa in that he gave a succinct verbal answer which matched his written answer. Gregory appears to have used a form of trial and improvement, first arriving at a pair of numbers with the correct total but incorrect difference and then adapting them until they met both criteria. His spoken answer adds little to his written answer but confirms the method and suggests that he understands it. For most of the interview, Gregory seemed happy to listen patiently to Darren, who had a lot to say. Gregory did not seem to want or need to pursue the solution to this particular problem.

The interview does not really add to our knowledge of how Darren tackled the stickers question, but it does support the possibility that he did not understand how to answer it and just tried to write something which related to the numbers in the question and matched something he had been taught before. However, we learn about Darren's strategies for tackling hard questions in writing. He talks about a range of general strategies such as going on to the next page and going back, trying to remember what has been taught or simply trying his best. He ends by suggesting that even if you have no idea at all 'you just do it' and this may well have been how he approached the question. It is possible that Darren has been taught these strategies in revision sessions, though unfortunately he does not appear to recall any particular mathematical approaches. He seems philosophical about being asked to tackle work which has little meaning for him.

For most of the interview, the two boys did not interact much. The one exception is when Gregory suggests that pictures can help you to tackle a problem and Darren picks up and expands on this point. Reference back to the last page of the written test showed that both boys had ticked the statement 'I like explaining things in writing' and Gregory had also ticked 'I like explaining things by talking'. Neither ticked the statement saying that they find explaining hard.

## Listening to Joe and Ben

Joe and Ben, who chose to be interviewed together, both gave the common incorrect answer of 38 in the written paper. Joe had provided a brief written explanation: $22 + 38 = 60$. Ben's written method was:

- 30 30 + 8 = 38

Later, when the interviewer asked for general comments on the written questions, Joe initiated discussion on stickers.

> Question number 3. I got it wrong. I don't understand... well, because 38 isn't 8 more than 22 and Jenny has 8 more stickers than Hilary.

Ben was then drawn in to the discussion by the interviewer.

> Well, I took away 30 and then I added 8 to the 30, which equals 38.

After some probing, Ben said that he thought Hilary had 30 and Jenny had 38. At this point, Joe joined in:

> Hilary couldn't have 30 because that would make 68... so that would make Hilary to have 22, that would make 60 but 38 is... wouldn't go... cos... it's 10 more than 22. Well, I've tried thinking about it but I can't... I still can't get anything.

The interviewer asked Ben whether he was happy with his answer of 38 and he said he was.

## What can we learn from Joe and Ben?

Again, much of the discussion was between the interviewer and individual children rather than between the children themselves. However, there was at least one point where the children were interacting with each other and not just with the interviewer. This was where Joe responded to Ben's justification of 38 by explaining why he didn't think this was possible. Ben was like many children interviewed in wishing to stick to his written answer but Joe showed in the interview that he was not happy with this answer. Yet he did not carry through any modified approach to get a different answer.

The interview showed that Joe had taken the important step of trying to work out the number of stickers that both girls had and then checking these numbers against the two constraints. As a result, he had realised that his answer was not possible. His interview therefore revealed more about his response to the question than his written answer. This could be because he did not write down everything that occurred to him on the answer paper. It could also be because the idea of checking and the doubts this led to only occurred to him during the interview. He may have had these thoughts between the written paper and the interview. At the end of the discussion Joe still seemed puzzled, whereas Ben seemed happy with his incorrect answer, although he had not engaged in the discussion in depth.

## Listening to Timothy and Mark

Timothy and Mark were interviewed about a week after they had completed the written paper. The pairing was carefully chosen by their teacher and there was good interaction between the two boys throughout the interview. Each listened to what the other was saying and responded accordingly. Timothy had put a wrong answer of 38 in the answer box but his working included the correct answer and finished with $34 + 26 = 60$. In his answer box Mark had written 38, then 34, both of which were crossed out and finally, 38 again but not crossed out.

The discussion was initiated by Mark when the interviewer asked for general comments.

I found this one quite hard, actually ... well. I didn't exactly know what to do. To add 4 on to Jenny's stickers or take away 4 off Hilary's and to take away 4 off Hilary's stickers or just add 8 on to Jenny's ... or take away 8 from Hilary's.

The interviewer pointed out that he had two answers originally, one of them crossed out. Timothy then entered the discussion.

I had 38. Well I worked out it was wrong to start with but then put the right ans...

Mark asked Timothy what answer he had put and Timothy replied '38'. The interviewer drew Timothy's attention to his crossed-out working. At this point both boys spoke at the same time, making it difficult to interpret their words though Timothy referred to the numbers 8 and the 4 and then clearly said:

So I worked out the 8 difference... add them together to make sure the answers were right, so... 60.

The interviewer asked about the 38 Timothy had put in the final answer box of his written response. There was a pause. Mark asked whether that was wrong, although he himself had the answer 38 and there had been no indication that this was not the correct answer. As Timothy now seemed doubtful about his answer of 38, the interviewer directed his attention to his working out where he suggested that one girl has 34 and the other 26.

Oh yes, I didn't really put that there'd be 8 different.

The interviewer asked whether there was 8 difference between the two numbers while pointing to the 26 and 34. Timothy said that there was and the interviewer asked whether he thought that this was now the right answer. He said 'yes'. Mark, however, disagreed and said:

I don't think it was because if you only add 8 on to there...

Timothy interrupted and Mark soon agreed with him:

Timothy: Oh no, it would be 34.

Mark: Yes, 34 because if you add on 8 there [pointing to the number 30] then you've got 30 add 38, which doesn't make 60, makes 68.

## What can we learn from Timothy and Mark?

Most of the discussion with Timothy and Mark about stickers is recorded above. It is clear that they spent much longer discussing this question than the other children did. Another major difference is that the two boys were engaging directly with each other at some points and did not always need the interviewer's intervention. They appeared to use the interview to rethink their answers rather than simply give an oral explanation of what they had done in the written paper. They were successful in doing this and by the end of the interview they had both moved from incorrect answers to the correct one. It may be that the way they tried to justify and explain their reasoning to each other in the interview helped them to do this. Significantly, both had already considered 34 as an answer at some stage. The interview seemed to give them an opportunity to clarify their thoughts and try to reach agreement on the correct answer.

## Reflecting on the interviews
### What we learned about the question

The interviews supported much of what we had already learned about the question and surmised about the children's thinking from earlier phases of the research. In particular, we were able to see some of the ways children of these ages went about solving it. A good example of this was Melissa's method, which was direct and based on the structure of the problem. In addition, the interviews supported our view that this particular question caused conflict in the minds of many children. This often resulted in children wanting to talk about this question, which was raised in discussion far more times than the other questions the children had completed in writing.

### What we learned about the thinking

The interviews also helped us learn a little more about those children who gave incorrect answers. For example, Joe seemed aware that his answer did not meet the constraints of the problem. Ben, on the other hand, was able to explain how he reached his incorrect answer but showed no wish to revise it. Leila was either unable or unwilling to explain how she had arrived at her incorrect answer. This variety of attitudes and confidence in incorrect answers could only be explored by

111

listening to the children: it was not evident in their written explanations and could not be deduced from them.

## What we learned about individual responses

Researchers sometimes use interviews as a tool to investigate written answers in the assumption that more will be revealed about what children did and why. Our findings suggest that this was not always the case. Leila, for example, declined to add anything about how she had arrived at her answer. We are likely to learn more about this from her written answer and by examining it carefully in relation to the question. It could therefore be argued that her spoken response tells us less than her written answer, or that it provides important information about her level of confidence and enthusiasm. In some cases the spoken and written responses were similar. Melissa is an example of this: she used the interview for reporting what she had done on the written paper rather than for adding anything. Joe is a good example of someone who tells us more in the interview than in the written paper. He reveals that he has found a way of checking the answer and has realised that it can't be correct. He is moving away from the reporting mode of Melissa's interview towards the re-thinking mode demonstrated by Timothy and Mark. Unfortunately, Joe made little overt progress with the re-thinking, as he could not find a way of moving beyond his difficulties. Timothy and Mark used the interview not just for reporting but for re-thinking: this allowed them to arrive at a correct answer.

## What we learned about paired interviews

The three examples show how the paired interviews operated in quite different ways. Melissa and Leila did not move beyond reporting on their written answers, neither did they really engage with each other: they both spoke in response to the interviewer. Joe and Ben behaved in a similar manner, though they showed signs of moving towards re-thinking the problem and towards interacting with each other. Timothy and Mark behaved quite differently: they engaged with each other and with the problem and were able to re-think the problem and arrive at the correct answer. It is interesting to speculate on why this is the case for these two boys but not for the other pairings. A possible explanation could lie in the pairing itself: the boys were used to working together or perhaps had similar ways of approaching mathematical tasks or similar levels of attainment. Another possible explanation is that both were already considering two possible answers to the question, including the correct one. It may be that the paired interview gave them the opportunity to explore ideas they had already started to consider. Whatever the reason, both we and Timothy and Mark were able to learn from listening to one another.

## What we learned about children's preferences and strategies

Of the eight children considered here, only Darren talked in detail about approaches to questions, though some of the other children interviewed spoke about their preferences. The statements at the end of the written paper also gave us some information which was surprising. Of the eight children, six ticked the statement 'I like explaining things in writing' but not 'I like explaining things by talking'. The two exceptions were Gregory, who ticked both boxes, and Ben, who ticked neither. None of these children ticked 'I find explaining hard'. This is a small group but the result nevertheless suggests that explaining things in tests was not such an ordeal for these children as we might assume. Nor was explaining by talking an easy option.

## Issues to think about

As researchers we were interested in how children responded to opportunities to explain their thinking verbally. We were also interested in whether pairing children encouraged them to listen to each other and whether they took serious notice of solutions arrived at by other children. For teachers, the issue of encouraging children to explain their mathematical reasoning to each other is also important. We include some suggestions for teachers to consider if they wish to create learning opportunities in the classroom:

- How often do your learners have the opportunity to talk about and reflect on their work?

- How can learners be encouraged to talk and listen to each other?

- How often do you listen to individual learners?

- How can a conjecturing atmosphere be fostered so that learners feel confident to talk about their work even when they are not confident they are right?

- How do you arrange your listening groups? In pairs, in small groups?

- How are the pairs or groups arranged? By friendships, by ability, by gender, by degree of confidence?

- What kind of questions do you use to get a discussion started and what prompts might you use to explore children's responses further?

## Conclusion

To return to the question in the title: we did learn more from interviews than from written answers. In some cases, methods were confirmed and we also gained insight into how confident children were about their answers. In particular, we realised that for many children the incorrect answer of 38 was not just a careless mistake but a solution which made sense. Children had a tendency to use the interviews to report on what they had done rather than to re-think it and sometimes wished to defend an answer they felt committed to rather than being open to a different solution.

We therefore wonder whether children might be more willing to share ideas when working verbally on a question from scratch rather than one they have already completed in writing some time previously. We reached new understandings by interviews conducted some time after written answers were provided and we feel that these positive results might be amplified by working verbally on questions.

## References

Arksey, H and Knight, P (1999) *Interviewing for Social Sciences: An Introductory Resource with Examples.* London: Sage Publications Ltd

Evens, H and Houssart, J (2004) Sum and Difference Problems at Key Stage 2. *Proceedings of the British Society for Research into Learning Mathematics* 24(2) Proceedings of the day conference held at the University of Leeds, June 2004 pp21-26 available from http://www.bsrlm.org.uk accessed September 2008

Houssart, J and Evens, H (2005) Giving examples and making general statements: two odds always make an even (in maths). In D. Hewitt and A. Noyes (eds) *Proceedings of the sixth British Congress of Mathematics Education held at the University of Warwick*, pp65-72

Mason, J with Graham, A and Johnston-Wilder, S (2005) *Developing Thinking in Algebra.* London: The Open University in association with Paul Chapman Publishing

# 9

## Pupils' perceptions of setting

### Barbara Allen

### Introduction

This chapter is concerned with the views of 10 to 11 year olds who were interviewed as part of a larger study exploring pupils' perspectives on their mathematics classrooms.

The research is unusual because it uses only data collected from pupils whereas other researchers working in this field tend to collect data from a variety of sources. I was concerned only with what the pupils perceived their mathematics classrooms to be like and therefore chose not to interview their teachers or to observe them in their classrooms. I was interested in what the pupils perceived to be taking place and how this influenced them, rather than checking the validity of their statements through standard methods of triangulation.

Semi-structured interviews were conducted with small groups of pupils, usually in twos or threes. Nine girls and nine boys self-selected into the project from across the three mathematics sets. I used prompts and probes to encourage them to talk about their experiences. These either involved specific questions or drawing and sorting tasks. The interviews were recorded and analysed using a grounded theory approach (Glaser and Strauss, 1967). I named the school Marsden Middle School and all pupils' names are pseudonyms that they chose.

One issue the pupils talked about was the organisation of their mathematics lessons. There were three classes in each year and pupils were put into sets for mathematics lessons. The use of setting in schools continues to be a contentious topic, yet there has been little consideration of the pupils' perspective. I consider a group of pupils' perspectives on setting and its impact on them as learners of mathematics. I discuss what we can learn from these pupils and the implications for primary mathematics classrooms.

## What does research say about setting?

In 1998, Ofsted reported that setting in primary schools could result in the polarising of the quality of teaching (Ofsted, 1998). Better quality teaching was evident in the highest mathematics sets and the poorest teaching in the lowest sets. Ofsted attributed this to the fact that the mathematics co-ordinator or specialist frequently taught the highest set. In the same year, Sukhnandan (1998) reported that this belief in the efficacy of setting was not supported by their review of research. Results from studies by Slavin in elementary schools (1987, 1990) and Boaler in secondary schools (1997) have shown that there is no difference overall between pupils' attainment in mixed ability or setted lessons. One of the main arguments against setting is the risk of labelling the pupils. There is also the risk that teachers will have lower expectations of pupils in the lower ability sets (Gregory, 1984).

If there is no conclusive evidence that any one form of grouping pupils is the most effective for raising standards then why are more and more primary schools in England setting pupils for mathematics lessons? It could be that the push for whole class teaching as a result of the Numeracy Strategy is the reason. Arranging pupils in ability sets in mathematics enables teachers to work with the whole class. Since the warnings by Ofsted in 1998, the number of schools that set primary school pupils in mathematics lessons has increased but the pupils' attainment has started to plateau. This has not affected the government's belief in the efficacy of setting.

In July 2007, Sir Peter Williams was asked by the Secretary of State to review the teaching and learning of mathematics in primary schools. In his Final Report (2008), Williams made no recommendations about the organisation of teaching groups but stated that pupils were entitled to access to the full mathematics National Curriculum and that setting can result in those in the lower sets being offered a restricted mathematics curriculum.

Setting is a contentious issue which has been debated for many years. Whilst researchers attempt to establish the most effective grouping for pupils, successive UK governments hold on to the ideology that setting is necessary. What do the pupils say about the impact of setting on them? How can primary school teachers use the results of what they say in organising their mathematics lessons to increase pupils' attainment?

## Marsden Middle School

Marsden Middle School was organised in years and classes and in sets for mathematics and English. The size of the sets was based on the belief that there should be fewest pupils in Set 3. This could result in Set 1 being quite large, sometimes with 32 pupils. Pupils were allocated to sets based on teacher assessment and sometimes on an internally written and administered test. It was not clear to me how much credence was given to teacher assessment or whether test results were paramount. Some pupils such as Abbie felt that basing the decision on tests results could be flawed.

> Abbie: ... maybe on that day when we took the test to see what set we were in then maybe that was just a really good day. That was a subject we knew about. (Set 1)

Working on Abbie's principle, it seems equally likely that a pupil could have a bad day and be put in a set that they thought was inappropriate. This allocation to a wrong set would not have been a problem if the sets were fluid. However, in the five terms that data were collected not one pupil moved between sets. It appeared that once they were allocated to a set, they stayed there for their middle school life. The pupils explained some of this lack of movement as organisational restrictions.

> Connor: The work in the middle set was too easy for me and Tim and they didn't have enough room in top set so we had to stay in middle. (Set 2)

The organisation of the pupils into sets was entirely in the hands of the teachers who, however, had outside forces in the form of published league tables, acting on them. The setting of the pupils was imposed by an external authority (the teachers) but it impacted on how pupils perceived themselves as successful or unsuccessful learners of mathematics.

Pupils raised these issues in the interviews:

- the impact on pupils of being put in a set;
- the impact on pupils of staying in a set and
- the impact on pupils of the classroom organisation in a set.

## The impact on pupils of being put in a set

The pupils were allocated to sets at the beginning of Year 6. Some were put in a set which they believed was appropriate:

> Guy: Well if we're put in sets then that's the set for us. We can't be stupid if we are in top set. (Set 1)

> Abbie: I always felt quite good about myself when I went into top set. I didn't sort of boast about it but at home I was really proud of myself. (Set 1)

> Alan: I was cheerful when I found out I was in top set maths. (Set 1)

> Connor: I reckon they should have a set which you feel comfortable in. ... And ... the right set for me would be middle, which I'm in now. (Set 2)

If the pupils were placed in a set where they felt comfortable, it confirmed their feelings about themselves and helped to create a positive personal identity. The comments the pupils made often contained some affective response, indicating that this positioning made them proud or cheerful. There were, however, some pupils who appeared baffled by their positioning.

> Caroline: I'm absolutely rubbish at maths even though I'm in top set. (Set 1)

Although, during data collection, Caroline accepted her position in Set 1 she continued to express the opinion that she was 'rubbish at maths'. Her continued position in Set 1 did not change this opinion of herself as basically an unsuccessful learner of mathematics. Gus was even more confused by his allocation to a set.

> I wasn't stupid when I was a 5th year, they put me in bottom set. (Set 3)

His comments show that his position in 'bottom set' made him believe that he was now 'stupid'. He was beginning to see himself as an unsuccessful learner purely because of his position in Set 3. He had started to question and alter his perceived identity, whereas Caroline did not alter her perceived identity as an unsuccessful learner of mathematics, when she was positioned in Set 1.

For the Set 1 pupils their positioning did much to boost their self-esteem. For those who felt they were in the correct set, like Guy, it confirmed their view of themselves as able to do mathematics. However, for some girls, like Caroline, who were less sure about their ability to do mathematics, their position in Set 1 put additional strain on them.

## The impact on pupils of staying in a set

Pupils come to know whether they are successful learners of mathematics through their interactions in the classroom and how they perform within a particular set. In forming these identities they are constantly making judgements about their performance and their positioning within the set. These judgements are not within their authority; they are reliant on the authority of the teacher who marks and comments on their work. In this situation the pupils have no voice and are effectively silenced. Although many Marsden pupils accepted the set in which they were placed, they had no control over the decision. Even if they felt they performed well in class, they were in no position to alter the set they were in.

A problem reported only by the Set 1 pupils, particularly the girls, and by Boaler (1997) was the additional pressure on them to maintain or improve their position. Since they were in the top set, the only way to improve their perceived position was by competing to perform better within the set. They appeared to be constantly comparing themselves to others in the set in order to verify their position and to ensure that they were not dropping down the pecking order.

> Sarah: I try and do my best so that I don't go down a set because I know I can't go up a set. ... Instead of getting into the next set up you're getting into the top of the year really, aren't you? ... It's nice to feel that you are better than some people below you. It's nicer to feel that you are not the bottom person. (Set 1)

> Caroline: Say you forget about the other sets and there's just your set you wanna be somewhere near the top, don't you? ... You feel you've achieved something as long as you are not at the bottom. (Set 1)

Natalia: I mean we're split into groups because we're all at different standards but I think in each set there is another different standard. There's the boffins and there's the lower ones. ... Lucy is like really good at maths but she writes it down really, really slowly and everything and so people class her as like quite bottom 'cos she never gets to finish the work and she likes everything to be perfect and pristine and everything. (Set 1)

Abbie: I know we're meant to be in top set, and we're meant to keep the standard up, but I sometimes think we get just as confused as other people do. And sometimes she [teacher] takes it for granted we know what we're doing, and we don't always know what we're doing. (Set 1)

By recognising that they were members of a particular set the pupils were also identifying themselves as not being members of the other sets. Although some of the girls (Caroline in particular) felt that their position in Set 1 was unstable, they still felt that this position had resonance with their personal identity. They saw themselves as being Set 1 pupils. But this identification of themselves had not resulted from complex interactions within a community; it was the result of a decision by an external authority. In a position of silence, the pupils did not recognise that they had an individual identity; their identity existed as part of a group.

An over-riding fear for the Set 1 pupils appeared to be the prospect of being moved down a set:

Sarah: I thought I was really going to get into trouble for not doing that homework.

Caroline: You might find she might move you down or something. (Set 1)

Nick: Failure could be like when you get dropped a set. (Set 1)

It seemed to me that part of their identity came from the complex meanings they attributed to being in Set 1 and not in Set 2 or Set 3, which included the persistent threat of moving down a set. Any change in their positioning within or between sets would cause dissonance as displayed by Gus when he was placed in Set 3. It appears that the pupils perceived a threat of being moved down a set even though they had never known it to happen.

The girls felt they had little control over their future in the set because they were given no opportunity to speak about their work and ideas.

Although they could work hard, they had no perception of their relative success or failure because their identities were affected by their positioning and this was in teachers' control. Whatever set the pupils were positioned in they had no control over the situation. In some cases, this included the physical position they had in the classroom.

## The impact on pupils of the classroom organisation in a set

The pupils in Set 1 talked about the seating arrangements in their mathematics classroom, giving an insight into the effect that these arrangements had on the pupils. Choosing where to sit in a classroom is often out of pupils' control because teachers use seating as a way of controlling pupils' behaviour. A variety of seating arrangements is used in schools: boy next to girl; sitting in alphabetical order; in chronological age. If one of these systems is used it is unlikely that a pupil will end up seated next to a friend. There was no evidence that any particular method was used by the teacher to seat the pupils in Set 1 but many still ended up sitting apart from their friends. Although they were not clear about how this situation had occurred, they appeared to accept it as the norm:

> Alan: They [boys] normally sit on a table and sometimes me and my friend we sit in front of them or sometimes there are like 2 tables put together, and Jim sits across the table from us. ... Girls are like sitting in the corner. (Set 1)

> Guy: ... they [girls] always sit in the corners and don't do anything. ... They're over the other side of the room. They don't answer things. (Set 1)

> Jane: Also in our classroom it's split in two because on one side there's loads of boys ... (Set 2)

This conversation between Abbie, Natalia and Sarah gives some idea of how seating arrangements came about and how the pupils accepted them as the *status quo*:

> Abbie: We're in different halves though. Say that's the classroom, she [Natalia] sits over there and I sit over here.

> Natalia: There are two different sides. We divide the classroom into two. I'm on one half, she's on the other.

> Abbie: There's like an aisle in the middle and Miss's desk is there.

> Sarah: Miss's desk separates the two.

121

Abbie: It's got nothing to do with who we're friends with, it's just the way we sit and that's the way we sit.

Natalia: It's just natural.

Abbie: It's got nothing to do with who we're friends with. Because there are a lot of people that we wouldn't usually be friends with but because we're sitting near them. (Set 1)

The physical separation of the boys and girls in the classroom appeared to result in a lack of awareness of how other groups were learning. If personal identity is formed as a result of negotiated experience and community membership then these pupils were only aware of part of the community and only involved in part of the experience (Wenger, 1998). The perception of both boys and girls was of a room divided by an invisible separator – in this case an 'invisible wall' (see Abbie's comment below). This separation also led to territoriality, with each group defending their physical position:

Guy: The boys sit next to the window, there's eight boys and we work together mainly, more or less. And we don't argue and other people don't really come and talk to you. ... They're [girls] over the other side of the room so we don't really know [if they are chicken to do things]. (Set 1)

Sarah: Because you don't talk to somebody on the opposite side of the classroom. ... We always line up on different sides as well. And different sides of Miss's desk half the time.

Abbie: It's like an invisible wall down the half.

Natalia: Just down the middle of Miss's desk. (Set 1)

Natalia: I'm not on the actual side of the maths class where there's a lot of boys. There's two boys on my side of the class and you don't really get a great insight into this boys' thing. (Set 1)

The pupils were building perceptions of people on the other side of the room based on their behaviour but admitted that they had little real insight into what was happening. It seemed that pupils were not only becoming aware of their own identities but were also projecting a particular identity onto other people. These perceptions were powerful and led some boys to believe that the girls were too 'chicken' to answer questions.

Their mathematics classroom was one where the only movement was when they got their work marked at the teacher's desk. Paechter (2000, p13) found that 'students repeatedly characterised the differences between subjects in terms of physical freedom or constraint; subjects were marked as those in which one could talk or move around or, conversely, in which one had to stay still at one's desk'. For most of the time the Marsden pupils were required to stay in the same place. This was not just in single lessons but their physical place in the classroom remained the same over a long period of time.

The Set 1 pupils described a classroom arrangement that had variety: some tables were sited singly whilst others were organised in groups of two or more. Cohen and Manion (1981) found that a rectangular arrangement of tables resulted in a tendency for pupils to interact more with each other and less with the teacher. This was the case for the Marsden pupils, who interacted with peers on their table but not with others in the room. The classroom organisation meant that some boys came to perceive the girls as silent or silenced within the classroom. If the pupils had been able to choose where they sat, their vision of their own and others' identities might have been different.

## The implications of setting: authority and control

All of the setting issues for the Marsden pupils were related to authority. They were placed in sets by an external authority (teachers), their success as learners of mathematics was judged by an external authority (teachers), and they were positioned in classrooms by an external authority (teachers).

This put pupils in a position of silence where they 'felt they had no control over the way that lessons were planned or conducted. They could not see a situation where they might have any control or where they could express any opinion. Their position as a successful or unsuccessful learner of mathematics depended entirely on the feedback they got from their teacher' (Allen, 2006, p89). This was compounded by the external authority exerted over pupils when the pupils 'recognised that the teachers were making decisions about their position as learners of mathematics but were unable to assess whether this was appropriate or not. Pupils supported the *status quo* and a view that mathematics is right or wrong.' (Allen, 2006, p.90).

The classroom practices and expected performances in particular sets were so deeply embedded that the pupils did not feel able to behave in a different way. They did not seem to have any view of themselves as agents within the classroom and could not envisage making changes. Even when they did suggest changes during the interviews these were about changes that teachers could make to their pedagogy rather than any change that could come from the pupils within the culture.

However, at the end of Year 6, there was some suggestion that a few Set 3 pupils were starting to feel the need for some personal authority and independence. This emerged during interviews before and after the end of Key Stage Tests (SATs). Under normal conditions pupils' work was quite varied and not always from textbooks or worksheets. However, when the SATs were imminent the sort of work chosen by the teacher changed:

> Gus: We just do it on sheets now, we don't do it in our maths books. We have this folder and we have to put the sheets in. (Set 3)

An aversion to external authority appeared in comments by Set 3 pupils in the build-up to the SATs. The pupils reported that their teacher exerted increased control over the work they did. The teachers were altering the curriculum and their pedagogy because of the pressure of the SATs (Webb, 1993). It was this increase in control that caused conflict for some pupils.

> Gus: ... but since we've been working on sheets, we have to go up to her and then she marks them. But when we had the maths books we just gave them in and then she marked them. So we are let down on some work, 'cos there's a long queue. ... so we get less done. (Set 3)

> Jo: I can't remember what we was doing but I was really enjoying it and miss always stops us and says and do this and do that and do that and I really wanted to do it and I felt really anxious to do it. Like sitting there watching Miss doing it again, and we already know what we are doing. She's still giving another example if people find it hard, we really like it and some people don't know how to do it. And I know how to do it sometimes and I feel really anxious to do it but she kept on talking. (Set 3)

The pupils were no longer content with the work the teacher was select-ing but did not want to decide for themselves what they should be do-ing. They wanted the teacher to fulfil the role they perceived as

124

appropriate. What was missing was the feeling that they themselves could effect change within their classrooms. They had no feeling of power and did not see that power was based on relationships but as invested in the external authority of teachers.

What the Marsden pupils were reporting was different from what was reported by teachers or researchers. External authority dominated their lives in a variety of forms. It is not surprising that these pupils started to question external authority. Research suggests that this questioning of authority emerges at a later stage, often amongst 14 to 16 year olds and may result in disaffection (Boaler, 1997). This research suggested that this disaffection, a consequence of a lack of personal authority, can start much earlier.

## Conclusion

Setting in mathematics lessons has been and still is encouraged by the government with an increase in setting in Key Stage 2 (Askew *et al*, 2001). The practice is growing, even though there is little research evidence to show that it improves pupils' attainment.

If an increase in mathematics attainment is now reaching a plateau maybe it is time that mathematics education in schools is focused again on learning rather than teaching. This chapter shows how listening to pupils can give a teacher information about the impact of setting on their perception of their success as a learner of mathematics.

The use of setting in UK schools means that many pupils are separated from their chosen friends. Some Marsden pupils also felt isolated in their mathematics sets because they were not sitting near their friends. The current preference for setting in mathematics lessons runs counter to the wishes of the Marsden pupils and is counter to research evidence.

## References

Allen, B (2006) Pupils' perceptions of Mathematics Classrooms. Unpublished PhD Thesis, University of Birmingham

Askew, M (2001) Policy, practices and principles in teaching numeracy. What makes a difference? In P. Gates (ed) *Issues in Mathematics Teaching*. London: Routledge Falmer

Boaler, J (1997) *Experiencing School Mathematics Teaching styles, sex and setting*. Buckingham: Open University Press

Cohen, L and Manion, L (1981) *Perspectives on Classrooms and Schools.* London: Cassell Educational Ltd

Glaser, B and Strauss, A (1967) *The discovery of grounded theory.* New York: Aldine

Gregory, R P (1984) Streaming, setting and mixed ability grouping in primary and secondary schools: some research findings. *Educational Studies* 10(3) pp209-226

Office for Standards in Education (1998) *Setting in Primary Schools: a report from the Office of Her Majesty's Chief Inspector of Schools.* London: HMSO

Paechter, C (2000) *Changing School Subjects: Power, Gender and Curriculum.* Buckingham: Open University Press

Slavin, R E (1987) Ability grouping and achievement in elementary schools: a best evidence synthesis. *Review of Educational Research* 57(3) pp293-336

Slavin, R E (1990) Achievement effects of ability grouping in secondary schools: a best evidence synthesis. *Review of Educational Research* 60(3) pp471-499

Sukhnandan, L with Lee, B (1998) *Streaming, Setting and Grouping by Ability: a review of the literature.* Slough: National Foundation for Educational Research

Webb, R (1993) *Eating the Elephant Bit by Bit: the National Curriculum at Key Stage 2, final report of research commissioned by the Association of Teachers and Lecturers (ATL).* London: ATL Publishers

Wenger, E (1998) *Communities of practice: Learning, meaning and identity.* Cambridge: Cambridge University Press

Williams, P (2008) *Independent Review of Mathematics Teaching in Early Years Settings and Primary Schools, Final Report.* London: DCSF

# 10

## 'Listen, it's easy': children as teachers of counting

*Brian Dale, Elizabeth Ryder, Lisa Strong,*
*Jenny Houssart*

### Introduction

This chapter is similar to preceding chapters in that it is about adults listening carefully to children in the context of mathematical activity. But the difference is that here the purpose of listening is for the adult to learn something new from the child.

It arises from a task carried out as part of an in-service course for practitioners working in primary classrooms. Following a session about young children learning to count, course members were asked to learn to count in a language which was new to them. As only a week was allowed, it turned out to be no more than making a start at learning. Various approaches were suggested, with the favoured option being to learn from a child. What follows is drawn from three accounts by course members, Brian, Lisa and Elizabeth, as they learned to count from a child or children.

Some would say that these three made a brave decision in deciding to learn from a child, rather than taking the other options of learning from an adult or teaching themselves from a book or from the web. In an earlier chapter Dave Hewitt argued that it was perfectly acceptable for an adult to be in a position of learning mathematics from or alongside a child. Here, that idea is explored further as children are explicitly asked to teach an adult something new. The accounts acknowledge that some of the participants see this as an unusual situation involving certain pressures. However they also reveal an impressive range of strategies and qualities from the children doing the teaching, the adults learning from them and some others who find themselves involved. The accounts of the three adult learners are reproduced in full below, followed by some additional reflections.

## Brian's story

The task was to learn to count in another language up to twenty. I decided that as there were two German-speaking children in the school this would be a good choice. I had only a week to learn the numbers and only limited time during the school day. As I teach all day, I could only meet with the child for 30 minutes a day, over four days. Kleis (a pseudonym) is 10 years old and in year 6. His father is from Germany and his mother is Dutch.

Kleis seemed really excited that an adult wanted to learn to count in German: he told me he could count to fifty. He could not believe that a member of the teaching staff needed to ask a child for help to learn. Although he could recite the numbers and had a good accent, he could not always spell the numbers. With his permission, I took some brief notes during the sessions over the four days: the results are shown opposite in the table.

I found this task stressful for two main reasons: having to learn to count in German and being taught by a child in Year 6. Kleis had expectations: these were that adults who teach in a school should be able to count to twenty in German. I did feel sometimes that I was being judged by him: this was most obvious when he asked me, 'Shall we stop there Mr Dale?' This task made me aware of pressures that children might experience in learning to count, especially if their first language is not English. When my German counting teacher wasn't around, there was no one to ask about the German numbers and their order.

Table 1: Brian learns to count in German

| Day | Numbers to learn today | What the child says | My reactions and thoughts | Comments | Were the numbers learnt? Y/N |
|---|---|---|---|---|---|
| Thursday 11.45 – 12.15 | 1-5 | Mr Dale listen, it's easy, *eins, zwei, drei, vier* and then its *fünf*. That's how it goes up to five Mr Dale. | I tried to pretend I knew exactly what I was doing. I felt quite pressured as a teaching member of staff I wanted to appear knowledgeable to the children. | I remembered *eins zwei* and *drei* from my school days, so that was a start, just two more to remember today. | Yes, not too bad only another fifteen. |
| Friday 11.45-12.15 | 5-10. | Mr Dale do you remember the numbers from yesterday? Here's the ones from up to ten. *Fünf sechs, sieben, acht, erm... neun* and *zehn*. | I decided to start from the beginning, *eins, zwei, drei, vier, fünf, sechs, seven* oh I mean *sieben.* Then I stopped as I couldn't remember anymore. | The first seven numbers seemed ok to me, however I couldn't understand why I didn't remember eight (*acht*) as it sounds similar to English number. | No- numbers 1-7. |

| Day | Numbers to learn today | What the child says | My reactions and thoughts | Comments | Were the numbers learnt? Y/N |
|---|---|---|---|---|---|
| Monday 11.45-12.15 | 10-15. | Mr Dale shall we do one to ten again today? Ready *eins, zwei, drei............ zehn.* That's the whole ten Mr Dale. | Felt better that I was sticking to ten numbers for the time being. Perhaps another five tomorrow. | It was better only working with ten numbers today as I had a lot to do this morning. My mind was a little distracted today. | No- numbers 1-10. |
| Tuesday 11.45-12.15 | 1-20 (practise all numbers) | What numbers do you want to learn today Mr Dale? *Zehn, elf, zwölf, dreizehn.* Shall we stop there Mr Dale? | I replied 10-15 would be good. | I tried my best but I did feel my German teacher was getting a little bored and frustrated due to the fact that I couldn't remember the sequence of numbers. | No- 1-12 |

## Reflections on Brian's story
### Teaching approaches

The fact that Brian has tabulated most of his account makes it easy to compare the teaching approach used across the four days. On the first day Kleis takes a direct teaching approach, telling the learner what he needs to know, exhorting him to listen and even adding the encouragement that, 'It's easy'. By the second day his approach has been adapted slightly and Kleis starts by asking Brian if he remembers the numbers from the day before, though he fails to actually revise them, opting instead to introduce the next set of numbers. This approach is adapted again the following day when Kleis suggests revision of the numbers covered on previous days and then repeats those numbers. On the fourth and final day, a different approach again is adopted, where the teacher starts by asking the learner which numbers he would like to learn. It is hard not to be impressed by the shifting pedagogical approach of this ten year old boy.

### The learner's perspective

Despite the young teacher's impressive progress, the adult in the role of learner to feels some stress. This leads Brian to draw parallels with children who learn mathematics in languages which are not familiar to them. Guidance by the National Association for Language Development in the Curriculum, concerning the teaching of mathematics to 7-16 year olds, supports the view that frustrations can be felt by those learning mathematics in a language they only partially understand (NALDIC, 2008). It is likely that another key factor is the role reversal, which leads to the interesting question of whether we should be surprised at the idea of adults learning from children. In this example the adult has learned to count in German at least to some extent, so it is interesting that the final column heading: Were the numbers learnt? is answered 'No' on three days out of the four. This initially seems puzzling but makes sense when compared with the second column, which sets out the numbers to be learned on each given day. The learner has made progress every time but this has not quite matched what was intended. It is tempting to think of our current target-driven culture when reading this, and to feel that setting targets has led a learner to define himself as failing when by other measures he has succeeded.

## European number systems

Brian noted the similarity between the German and English numbers for 8 and this is also true for other numbers such as 6, 7 and 9. There are many similarities across European number systems; Table 2 provides number names in three European languages. This connection between number names and different languages is examined in detail by

| Numeral | English | French | German |
|---------|---------|--------|--------|
| 1 | one | un | eins |
| 2 | two | deux | zwei |
| 3 | three | trois | drei |
| 4 | four | quatre | vier |
| 5 | five | cinq | fünf |
| 6 | six | six | sechs |
| 7 | seven | sept | sieben |
| 8 | eight | huit | acht |
| 9 | nine | neuf | neun |
| 10 | ten | dix | zehn |
| 11 | eleven | onze | elf |
| 12 | twelve | douze | zwölf |
| 13 | thirteen | treize | dreizehn |
| 14 | fourteen | quatorze | vierzehn |
| 15 | fifteen | quinze | fünfzehn |
| 16 | sixteen | seize | sechzehn |
| 17 | seventeen | dix-sept | siebzehn |
| 18 | eighteen | dix-huit | achtzehn |
| 19 | nineteen | dix-neuf | neunzehn |
| 20 | twenty | vingt | zwanzig |

Table 2: number words in English French and German

Menninger (1969), who traces number names across a range of languages, ancient and modern. He uses the similarities to discuss the idea of linguistic affinity and this forms part of an argument which suggests that many languages may have a common root. For the many children who move between European countries, or who start to learn modern foreign languages at primary level, these similarities are helpful.

Wider similarities between many European number systems are discussed by Fuson and Kwon (1991), who contrast European systems of number words with their Chinese-based equivalents. They point out that whereas Chinese-based systems tend to be regular, European systems tend to be irregular. Irregularities in English number names are familiar to primary teachers. These include the fairly arbitrary words eleven and twelve, and the fact that teen numbers are spoken with the units first, but written with the ten first. As Brian discovered, the German numbers for 11 and 12 are similarly irregular and the later teen numbers also carry the *zehn* (10) at the end in a similar way to English. German numbers beyond 20 continue to be spoken and written in opposite ways, so for example 25 is *fünfundzwanzig* (5 and 20).

Other European languages also contain some interesting examples such as the French for 99, *quatre-vingt-dix-neuf* (4-20-10-9). These irregularities may mean that learning to count takes a little longer, but they have other consequences because the number names do not always make the number system of tens and units transparent. Fuson and Kwon (1991) therefore suggest that children who work in systems with irregular number names might have additional difficulties in early calculations compared with children who work in systems where the number names are purely logical; it is particularly important that children using irregular systems have access to representations such as tens and units and digit cards, which make the structure of numbers clear.

## Lisa's story

I chose to learn Bengali as it is the most widely spoken language both in my class and in my school.

I asked a nine year old girl to help me learn to count. I asked her to write the numbers down against the numeric symbols we use (1,2,3...); she did this at home with the help of her parents as she said she could only remember the numbers up to 5. The next day she brought in the piece of paper with the Bengali words next to the numeric equivalent. See table 3 for a typed version of the list she produced. At playtime I joined her in the playground so that she could teach me.

| Number | Word | number | Word |
|--------|------|--------|------|
| 1 | ek | 11 | egarro |
| 2 | dhoi | 12 | barro |
| 3 | teen | 13 | therro |
| 4 | char | 14 | sudo |
| 5 | phas | 15 | phonerro |
| 6 | soi | 16 | shullo |
| 7 | shat | 17 | shothro |
| 8 | aat | 18 | aataro |
| 9 | noiy | 19 | unnish |
| 10 | dhosh | 20 | bish |

Table 3: Child's list of Bengali number names.

She began by reading all the numbers to me really fast. I asked her to slow down and just tell me the first five numbers (in sequence) as a chunk, and then the next five. She read them out, then I repeated them. Once I had mastered this, she tested me by giving me the English name and I had to give the Bengali equivalent; we also did the reverse of this. I referred back to the paper with the words written down at first and made mental notes in my head about the numbers. Some of them reminded me of other words, like *char*, I remembered as tea, and *dosh-10* which reminded me of money. From being able to see the written word I was also able to make connections with the initial letter sounds eg *soi-6*. Lots of children came over to see what I was doing in the playground, which was quite intimidating as most of them were Bengali, so I had to try my hardest to get it right and pronounce the words correctly. They all had a go at testing me.

After learning the first ten numbers during break time, I was keen to learn up to 20. I practised counting in Bengali everywhere I went. I counted stairs, fingers, and in my head as often as I could and shared my new found knowledge with my colleagues. They were quite impressed. After lunch I attempted to learn the next ten. These were a little trickier to remember. I could not make any obvious connections or word associations, so I learnt them in smaller chunks of threes. The rhythm and similar-sounding words helped me to remember the numbers, as there was no obvious number pattern apart from the similar initial sounds of 1 and 11, and 8 and 18. For some words, I wrote my own way of pronouncing them in English next to the number.

The key factors that helped me to learn to count in Bengali were the opportunities I had to repeat and practise my counting for short periods of time as well as being able to move at my own pace. The child teaching me repeated the words to me often and corrected my pronunciation. This was beneficial to me: as without this support it would have taken me a longer time to learn this new number system, as I may have been saying the words incorrectly. She never tired of repeating words or correcting me when I got them wrong, and was really pleased when I managed to get them right. I also benefited from knowing the numbers in my own language before I began. This allowed me to make connections with what the words meant. This is also true for children who are multi-lingual if they know the numbers in their own mother tongue than the principles of learning other number names in different languages are similar (Griffiths, 2007).

All these experiences of learning to count in Bengali mirror those of a young child first learning to count. A good enthusiastic teacher is vital to a child or adult's desire to learn, as they give encouragement and can make the experience of learning enjoyable. Knowing a number system before I began also gave me an advantage over a young child, as I was able to use familiar words as well as word associations to help me. A child's language would be less developed at this stage of learning numbers so the child would not have the vocabulary to make these connections. As an adult, I was also able to write my own phonetic interpretation, which would not be accessible to a child of pre-school age.

## Reflections on Lisa's story
### Teaching and learning issues

There are some similarities between Lisa's account and that given by Brian. Both feature enthusiastic teachers who start too fast for their slightly anxious learners. In both cases the approach was soon modified and in Lisa's case this seems to have happened as part of a process of negotiation between teacher and learner. As learner, Lisa had a clear idea of what was making it difficult for her and what might help. The teaching was soon modified to meet her needs. Comparisons with more usual teaching situations are unavoidable, and raise several questions. The first is whether children as learners are able to identify what helps and what hinders their learning in the way that Lisa did. Related to this is the issue of how children can be encouraged to develop an understanding of what helps them to learn, which is only viable if they are aware of alternatives and if alternatives are available. The final and key question is to what extent children as learners are able to have a say in the way they are helped to learn mathematics.

Choosing to learn to count in Bengali presented Lisa with an additional problem that Brian did not have because of the different script. She overcame this by using the phonetic spelling of the number names, written at home by the child and her family. Producing this list was no mean feat for the child, as producing phonetic equivalents in another language is inherently problematic and different versions exist. The original hand-written list produced by the girl and her family hints at some of the issues that may have been raised as the word for 14 is represented in two different ways and the word for 15 starts with a *ph* and then *f* is suggested instead. Because the child was asked to write the numbers using the alphabet used in England, she was not able to make use of additional symbols and accents which featured in some transliterations of Bengali numbers (Radice, 1994, p202). Lisa's chosen number system was irregular between ten and twenty in the same way as many European systems. She did not have many similarities to help her in the way that Brian did, though a careful look at the phonetic spellings suggests some similarities between the Bengali and English words for 6, 7, 8, and 9. Menninger (1969) identifies some similarities between number words in languages which are not obviously linked. He uses this as part of his argument that the languages may have a common root in what he calls the 'Original Indo-European Language' (page 101).

## Children learning to count

Lisa's account points to the parallels between her experience and that of young children learning to count. A key issue in learning to count in any language is that the first ten words, at least, are apparently arbitrary names which just have to be learned, largely by repetition. Young children have to learn some other important things when learning to count; in particular they need to know the one-one principle, that each object to be counted needs to be matched with a number word, and the cardinality principle that the last number word in the count tells you how many objects you have (Gelman and Gallistel, 1978). The work of Griffiths (2007), as quoted above by Lisa, argues that children learn these important principles whatever language they count in and should therefore not be discouraged from learning number names in more than one language. Kenner (2004) provides examples of young bilingual children who learn to count in more than one language and also learn to record calculations using different numerals.

## Number symbols

In her account, Lisa uses the carefully chosen phrase 'the numeric symbols we use', also sometimes referred to as Hindu-Arabic (Land, 1960) or modern numerals. Some writers acknowledge the likelihood that the origins of modern numerals are Indian, although a detailed compilation of number systems by Ifrah (1998) indicates that the origin and evolution of number symbols is as complex as that of their names, as discussed earlier. A table is presented by Ifrah (1998, p384) which suggests that a large number of numeral systems derived from Brahmi. These are classified in different ways so that Bengali numerals are presented as being derived from Brahmi via Gupta and then Siddham, whereas modern numerals are derived from Brahmi via Gupta and then Nagari. Tamil numerals, to be discussed in the next section, are derived from Brahmi via another route. This argument would account for some of the similarities between numerals in different systems, while the considerable lapse of time and interaction between different cultures involved could account for the differences. However, as Ifrah points out, even if we accept that these various number systems originated in this way, it still leaves the question of how Brahmi numerals originated, and this is the subject of a range of possible explanations. A popular idea is that the first three numerals derive from one, two or three horizontal lines joined together, though it is harder to find explanations for the numerals 4 to 9.

## Elizabeth's story

As soon as this task was discussed, I knew immediately which language I would attempt to learn. In my year 5 class (9-10 year olds), there are two girls from Sri Lankan families. One was born in the United Kingdom, whilst the other girl came to this country two years ago. Both speak Tamil at home with English as their second language. Both girls were willing to help me with my task and became excited when we met for our first session during the lunch break.

To prepare for this task, I had found a phonetic spelling of the numbers from 1 to 10 on a website. The list shown in Table 4 was compiled starting with the list from the web and extended with the children's help. I was sure that this would help with my pronunciation, although the girls were in some disagreement about the correct pronunciation of some numbers. We began by looking at the phonetic transliteration and the girls took it in turns to say a number, which I repeated. I was looking for a pattern to help me and it was obvious that so far all the numbers ended in *u*. I enquired if this would be the case beyond the number 10 and was informed that all numbers ended in *u*. I was curious to know the significance of this ending: the girls had no explanation but seemed impressed that I was interested in their number system. I was told that one hundred was pronounced *nuhru*. 'Miss, are you going to learn Tamil?' Although I explained that I would not be trying to learn numbers beyond 20, both girls were willing to meet again and help me further.

However, lack of time prevented further instruction, but I was given a written explanation, as dictated by the father of the one of the girls, of the significance of the *u*. Had I pursued this task further, I would have approached it differently and put myself in the position of the pupils who were trying to learn English and used resources such as cubes, counters, or cards with written numbers. I certainly felt that repetition was key in learning to count – as well as having someone to check your counting.

| Number | Word | Number | Word |
|--------|------|--------|------|
| 1 | ondru | 11 | pynondru |
| 2 | irandu | 12 | pynirandru |
| 3 | moondru | 13 | pynmoondru |
| 4 | naangu | 14 | pynnaanygu |
| 5 | ainthu | 15 | pynainthu |
| 6 | aaru | 16 | pynaaru |
| 7 | aylu | 17 | pynaylu |
| 8 | ettu | 18 | pynettu |
| 9 | onpathu | 19 | pynonpathu |
| 10 | pathu | 20 | iravethu |

Table 4: Extended list of Tamil numbers

## Reflections on Elizabeth's story
### Teaching and learning approaches

Elizabeth's account echoes many of the points made by Brian and Lisa about useful strategies such as repetition. Elizabeth also raises the issue of the resources often used to help children to count. It is interesting to speculate which of these might help someone learning to count in their second language and which would be less helpful. This is linked to the aspects of counting identified by Gelman and Gallistel (1978) discussed earlier. Cubes, counters and other objects are particularly helpful in establishing one-to-one correspondence and also in providing sets of objects that we want to know the size of, hence introducing cardinality. For those familiar with these principles but seeking to learn to count in a new language, resources such as cards with written numbers on them are particularly useful. Elizabeth also mentioned web resources which can also be of great help to those learning to count in a new language, especially as many of them include sound. The website that Elizabeth used (EMAS, 2007) provided a number line in Tamil as well as phonetic transliteration of the number names into English. It included a facility to click on the number symbols and hear the words.

## Family involvement

Both Elizabeth and Lisa noted that the families of the children teaching them to count became involved in the activity in some way. This was partly to provide additional information about the number systems, though the children must have been sufficiently motivated by the activity to mention it at home. Family involvement seems particularly appropriate as it is acknowledged by many writers that learning to count is to a large extent a social activity, an issue which is discussed in Nichola Abraham's chapter earlier in this book. In the case of young children learning to count in bilingual families, informal activities in the home can often take place in different languages on different occasions (Griffiths, 2007). One illustration of an activity involving a school and families in investigating number systems is described by Emblen (1996). A year two class (6-7 year olds) collected number systems from around the world using the expertise of parents and families as a resource. Information on many number systems was collected in the form of written symbols and numbers spoken onto audio tape. The project was presented as both an opportunity to involve families in the curriculum and as a mathematical opportunity as children were able to explore similarities and differences in the systems and mathematical issues arising.

## The Tamil number system

Elizabeth noted some regularities in the Tamil number system and her handwritten list of the number names from 11-20 also suggested that these follow a much more regular pattern than the teen numbers in English or any of the other languages considered in this chapter. By reading across rows in Table 4, it can be clearly seen how the teen numbers as written by Elizabeth relate to the first ten numbers provided by the web site. In fact the Tamil system is logical and how numbers are said reflects the way they are written and their underlying structure. This is linked to the way the Tamil number system has evolved from an ancient one which preceded the place value or positional system and did not use zero. This, referred to as a hybrid number system by Ifrah (1998), involved expressing numbers long hand in terms of powers of tens. So the number 573 would be written in a form equivalent to five hundreds seven tens and three, with symbols for hundred and ten included. The system's evolution is described in detail by Ifrah (1998) and is summarised by Kaplan (2005). The ancient Tamil system is an interesting illustration of how modern number systems have evolved and also shows what a difference zero makes.

## Conclusion

We have considered some of the many points arising from the three accounts; the experience was rich in lessons on what happens when adults learn mathematics from children. The three accounts differ but all record largely positive outcomes. In all cases the teaching was adapted or negotiated in some way to meet the learner's needs. There was also in all accounts a shared responsibility both for trying to accomplish the set task and for trying to find ways of doing so. These factors are highly desirable in any learning situation and all children learning mathematics should be routinely treated in this way.

The week after these tasks were carried out, Brian, Lisa and Elizabeth brought their notes to the session to share with the rest of the group. Others in the group had learned to count in languages including Arabic, Spanish, Mandarin Chinese, Russian, Turkish, Portuguese, Albanian, Italian and Welsh. Some of these languages also presented problems of different transliterations and pronunciations. Some presented other challenges: there is more than one way of counting in Welsh and different words for the number 1 exist in several languages, depending on how the word is used.

Our discussions covered features of different number systems, uses of number aids and a growing admiration for children learning mathematics in an additional language or moving between languages on a regular basis. We also considered many general teaching and learning issues. In listing what helped and hindered in the task, we identified some common themes. The patience and enthusiasm of those doing the teaching was frequently mentioned. A key item on the wish list of these adult learners was a teacher who could be approached as many times as necessary for reminders, clarification or support. We suspect that children as learners might tell a similar story.

# References

EMAS (2007) Tamil Number Line with Tamil Audio, Portsmouth Ethnic Minority Achievement Service. http://www.blss.portsmouth.sch.uk/resources/tamline1_10.shtml accessed July 2008

Emblen,V (1996) Bilingual children learning number. In R. Merttens (ed) *Teaching numeracy. Maths in the primary classroom*. Leamington Spa: Scholastic

Fuson, K and Kwon, Y (1991) Chinese-based regular and European irregular systems of number words: The disadvantages for English-speaking children. In K. Durkin and B. Shire (eds) *Language in Mathematical Education, Research and Practice*. Milton Keynes: Open University Press

Gelman, R and Gallistel, C (1978) *The Child's Understanding of Number*. Cambridge, Massachusetts: Harvard University Press

Griffiths, R (2007) Young children counting at home. *Mathematics Teaching* 2003, p24-26

Ifrah, G. (1998) *The Universal History of Numbers, From prehistory to the invention of the computer*. London: The Harvill Press (translated by David Bellos, E.F. Harding, Sophie Wood and Ian Monk from the French edition published in 1994)

Kaplan, M (2005) Tamil Numbers, Unicode Technical Note. http://unicode.org/notes/tn21/tamil_numbers.pdf accessed July 2008

Kenner, C (2004) *Becoming Biliterate, Young children learning different writing systems*. Stoke on Trent: Trentham Books

Land, F (1960) *The Language of Mathematics*. London: John Murray

Menninger, K (1969) *Number Words and Number Symbols*. Cambridge, Massachusetts: MIT Press (translated by Paul Bronerr from the revised German edition published in 1958)

NALDIC (2008) Some issues concerning EAL in the mathematics classroom. http://www.naldic.org.uk/ITTSEAL2/teaching/Maths1.cfm accessed July 2008

Radice, W (1994) *Teach Yourself Bengali*. London: Hodder Education

# 11

## Latter day reflections on primary mathematics

### Jenny Houssart

### Introduction

This chapter deals with learners' views about primary school mathematics, an issue mentioned in several earlier chapters. In this chapter the views are given with the benefit of hindsight by adults aged 75 or older. It is not unusual to encourage adults to share their memories of learning mathematics at school. It is sometimes used as a device in teacher education programmes to encourage trainees to consider what factors helped or hindered their learning and to heighten their awareness of their own feelings towards mathematics (Crook and Briggs, 1991). Adults who return to learning mathematics later in life are also sometimes encouraged to share their mathematical life histories, which commonly start with their experiences at primary school. Sometimes adults experiencing difficulties with or anxiety about mathematics are encouraged to look at their early experiences of learning the subject in a search for possible reasons for their disaffection (Buxton, 1981).

The chapter is based on written accounts, stored at the Mass-Observation archive based at the University of Sussex. The archive specialises in gathering material about everyday life in Britain and much of this takes the form of answers to questions known as directives which are sent out several times a year to those taking part in the project. Most directives are composed of several questions or subjects which the writers are invited to respond to. In this case, the responses are to a question about number which was asked in the first part of the spring 2004 directive.

The question was about uses of and feelings about numbers and also invited writers to keep a Numbers Day Diary noting their use of number throughout a chosen day. In keeping with other questions asked in the contemporary Mass Observation project, it was written in a fairly open-ended way. Looking at the responses, we discovered that many writers, especially older ones, recorded their memories of school mathematics. A key issue in reading these accounts is that we are dealing with what people choose to tell us, sometimes about their own everyday life and about events many years in the past. Such data clearly has limitations if we wish to draw factual conclusions about peoples' experiences. Issues related to the use of data from this archive are discussed in detail by Bloome, Sheridan and Street (1993) and by Sheridan (1996). Nevertheless, the data is a rich source for gaining insight into the writers' attitudes and beliefs, the focus of this chapter.

The following sections look at extracts from the accounts of six older writers with particular emphasis on what they say about their own experiences of learning mathematics at primary or elementary school. The six were chosen partly in order to show a variety of views and ways of responding to the question and partly because they shed light on three key themes: using and applying mathematics; mental mathematics and mental agility and grandparents and mathematics. The chapter concludes by considering how the views of these writers and other older people may be relevant both to those working in primary schools today and more widely.

## A lifetime of using and applying mathematics

The first two writers considered, in common with others, were more interested in charting their use of mathematics across the years than in recounting mathematical encounters on a particular day. Both give the impression of being successful users of mathematics, or at least certain aspects of mathematics, throughout their lives.

## Bill's story

When these accounts were written in 2004, Bill was 80 years old. He started school in 1926 at the age of $3^1/_2$ and left in 1937 with no qualifications. Bill mentioned his experiences at school in both the opening and closing sections of his response. These are quoted below and, in common with other extracts used in this chapter, they are reproduced as far as possible with the original spelling and punctuation.

> I have always been good at mental arithmetic, at age 7 to 8 I was always top of the class of 50 pupils aged 7 to 9. It was a natural aptitude but it was assisted by being taught the tables up to 12 times 12. The weekly tests were also helpful. I was good at addition, subtraction, division and multiplication, decimals and percentages. I think the only sensible way to do well with numbers is to be taught thoroughly until properly understood. ...

> As you can see, I enjoy numbers and although I left school in 1937 when I was 14 I have invariably been better with numbers than my colleagues throughout my life. It is a natural aptitude. You can see I have to be careful with my spelling, but I am doing my best. I apologise for my poor handwriting but I am left-handed and I think more quickly than I can write. (Bill, age 80)

Only the opening and closing paragraphs of Bill's account are quoted here, but the whole account is extensive and talks in detail about how he has used mathematics throughout his life. In particular he writes about his use of numbers and measures during his career in the aviation industry, including discussion of conversion to metric units and of safety requirements. He also writes at some length about financial matters, including his unofficial role as pensions advisor to many of his colleagues.

## Yvonne's story

The next extracts are taken from Yvonne, a widow living with her family who gives her age as 80+. Like Bill, Yvonne claimed to have been good at mathematics throughout her life. Her account started with a description of her use and awareness of numbers during the early part of the day when she dressed and prepared her breakfast. She refers mostly to practical uses such as time and other aspects of measurement, though she also admits to silently counting to herself when carrying out certain activities although she 'cannot say why'. She also says she counts stairs when she goes up them, but never when coming down. She moves on to describe her attitudes to mathematics and to mention school mathematics in the second paragraph of her account, reproduced in full below.

> From an early age I have been fascinated by numbers and enjoy doing puzzles which involve figures. At school I enjoyed maths lessons (which were called arithmetic) so I naturally got a job doing calculations etc in the wages office of a large engineering plant. I had to work out piecework rates of pay, deduct Income Tax and Social Security payments. I loved my big ledgers with the columns of names and figures. Time fascinates me too, so I often time various things that I do. When shopping I am very glad that I am pretty good at mental arithmetic, as so many products are priced by the amount of the packet or can or bottle – 100 grams being the favourite. I have never used a calculator, finding it Quicker to do such sums in my head. I was amazed when a young lady at the cash desk rang up 85p four times for my light bulbs. (Yvonne, age 80+)

Yvonne's short account ends with some general reflections on numbers, including her success in remembering phone numbers and her lack of it in the Lottery.

### What can we learn from Bill and Yvonne?

Bill and Yvonne both share memories of a mathematics curriculum dominated by arithmetic, including recall of multiplication facts and practice of calculations. Like many respondents, Bill had only an elementary education which was common before the 1944 educational reforms initiating secondary education for all pupils. The curriculum his account suggests is consistent with what is known about the teaching of mathematics in elementary schools (Brown, 2001). Yvonne appears to have had similar experiences of learning mathematics, though she does not mention ages or types of schools.

These accounts suggest that both learners were satisfied with their experience of learning mathematics at school and have found it useful in their lives. Both view mathematics as useful and give examples of how they have deployed it in their everyday life and work. The examples are dominated by calculations carried out in the context of money and measurement. Both hint at the possibility that younger generations have not been given the useful grounding in arithmetic that they believe their generation received. This view was shared by other writers and is considered in more detail elsewhere (Houssart, 2006, 2007).

146

Despite what some might see as a limited education, Bill appears to have been a successful learner of mathematics at school. He opens his account by saying he has always been good at mental arithmetic and Yvonne also suggests that her fascination with numbers was present at an early age. In both cases their enthusiasm and aptitude appears to have been maintained throughout their lives. Although teaching is mentioned, Bill in particular tends to ascribe this to natural aptitude.

The key message of both accounts is that mathematics is useful for everyday transactions and for work. However Yvonne also mentions that she enjoys doing puzzles involving figures and in the early part of her accounts she writes about counting stairs and silently counting to herself. This less utilitarian aspect of mental arithmetic was mentioned by others and is explored in more detail in the next two examples.

## Mental mathematics and mental agility

The next two responses to be considered had some features in common with those described above, including examples of using mathematics in everyday contexts such as money. The writers considered below stuck more closely to the question than the first two and, as asked, structured their accounts around a particular day's events. Despite this, both still managed quite specific mentions of mathematics learned early in their schooling.

### Heather's story

Heather, at 91, was the oldest person to reply to the directive. Heather's account of her day suggests quite an active life in which numbers play a part. In the morning she visited the shops but spent the afternoon as she describes below. The second quotation, which includes a direct mention of school mathematics, is taken from the end of her entry.

> After dinner and watching a little TV, I settled down to a few games of patience – three types. I play against previous games & set myself targets of numbers of cards played to achieve a certain standard. If too low a score, I play that type again. If I complete the game, I do not play it again until the next night or whenever. I play patience for dexterity & against osteo. arthritis, and also the planning of the course of the game and numbers happen to come in this all the time. ...

> The best thing one of our teachers taught us was little short cuts involving 10s + 5s + 3s + the primary numbers. I don't play bridge, but crib is a very good game for adding and dividing & also dominoes, but not being a mathematician, I'm more likely to have words flitting about in my head! (Heather, age 91)

Heather's account ends there and we can only speculate about some of the details and whether by shortcuts she means divisibility tests and whether primary numbers should be prime numbers. Despite the lack of precision, her mention of a particular type of activity from her school days is no mean feat for someone old enough to have started school during the First World War.

## Roland's story

Roland was 81 at the time of writing. He started his account of one day at a very early point in the day:

> I find myself waking earlier and earlier these days. If I get up my wife is disturbed, both in the sense of being woken herself and of worrying whether I, who used to taste a lengthy course of near-death when I slept, am unwell. So I have devised one or two mental tricks to try to get back to sleep. They seldom work, but even so they keep my mind from pursuing all those dreadful thoughts which I know to my cost make the elderly depressed in the hours before dawn. One of these exercises is factorising numbers, and my day began in just this way.

> It is a simple concept, based largely on the mental arithmetic I was first taught when I went to the primary school at the age of 3 (*sic* – we were in a small village where the master knew every child and took each one as soon as he felt there would be an advantage to the child). You simply start counting from one, and when you reach four you state the factors of four i.e. two times two if you are very small or two squared if you are a bigger child. And so on until either you have fallen asleep or you are overcome by other, pressing, needs. (Roland, age 81)

Later in his account, Roland talks about using numbers for a variety of practical reasons. However, the example given above differs from this and suggests that there are benefits in being able to occupy one's mind by working with numbers. Despite this rather alarming start, Roland later reports that his wife has 'persuaded herself that I am indeed my usual self' and this is followed by a description of their joint shopping trip and an evening watching sport on television.

## What can we learn from Heather and Roland?

Heather and Roland do not identify as strongly with mathematics as the writers considered earlier, and Heather's account suggests she is more interested in words than numbers. Nevertheless, both appear fairly confident with basic arithmetic and engage in mental arithmetic by choice. Other writers give similar examples and mental arithmetic, other than for strictly functional reasons, seems to occur in three main ways. The first is the playing of games, including keeping scores, which could be seen as functional or recreational depending on one's viewpoint. The second is counting of steps or objects or just mental counting for no particular reason. The third appears to be deliberate attempts to do mathematics in order to keep the brain agile or occupied.

Several earlier chapters consider young children's views about why we count and draw on possible reasons given by Munn (1997). It is clearly positive that as children become older they become more aware of the practical applications of counting and calculating. Despite this, it is interesting to note that the older people considered here do count or calculate without needing to 'know how many'. The idea of counting and calculating for themselves appears important to many in this age group. Keeping the brain active and healthy is seen as important by many respondents and it appears that mathematics has a part to play in this. One interpretation of this is as an ultimately useful activity.

A final commonality of the two accounts above is the claim to remember specific details from school mathematics many years later. Although we cannot check their accuracy, the claims themselves are impressive and provide a contrast to many teachers' concerns that pupils do not remember what they learn from one day to the next.

## Mathematics and grandparents

Many respondents were grandparents and at least one was a great grandparent. Grandchildren, like other family members, were sometimes mentioned in passing, for example in the context of birthday cards or phone calls. In the two examples considered below, the role of the writers as grandparents was more central to at least parts of the accounts.

## Henry's story

Henry described himself as a retired typesetter and a part-time main-tenance assistant in the family hotel and bed-sit business. He was a widower with three children and fourteen grandchildren. Henry started his account with references to numbers earlier in his life, including mentions of his time at sea and of having to remember his mother's co-op number when going shopping – a number he could still recall at the time of writing, having forgotten many numbers encountered more re-cently. He moved on to describe his encounters with numbers through-out the day, including a short paragraph about his grandchildren. Later in the account he returns to this subject and later still in his extensive report Henry mentions his own schooling. The relevant extracts are re-corded below.

> As it was a school day, I popped round to see my grandchildren off to school. Although I did not have anything to do with numbers then, I checked that one of them had the maths I was helping him with the day before. All long divi-sion, ten problems...

> When I pick the three boys up from school, the five year old comes out early and I do his 'homework' for 45 minutes and his book was about a farmer who kept loosing and finding sheep in different places and we needed to know how many sheep he had at one time. Although the total was never more than one digit, it was still difficult for him, as he had to remember each time how many sheep were in each place.

> After I got them home, their mother was out at work, but luckily the other boys did not have any maths homework so I did not have to deal with numerals as I usually do...

> I am astounded that the UK kept the imperial measurements for so long and often wondered why it was ever invented. The waste of time I spent as a child calculating tons, 20 cwts, 4 qtrs, 2 stones, 14 lbs, 16 ozs, etc. It was not until we decimalised that I wondered if industry did what we had to do at school. We were given several weights in all these units and had to total them up by entering each item under its respective column and dividing the base unit (i.e. 16oz) and carrying the lbs. over to the lb column. It took ages to do. Linear was the same with their inches, feet, yards, rods, chains, furlongs and miles.

> We were taught a number of things to do in arithmetic when I was at school, and at the time some of the subjects did not seem to be of great use. My

grandson came home with problems of factorising and could not understand how it was done. It dawned on me that I had never needed the knowledge at any time anyway and wondered why we needed to do it and it took some time for me to find out how to do it. I have since found out one of its uses, and that is to find the lowest common denominator for fractions, but none of my clever friends could remember the way to do it. (Henry, age 78)

Henry follows these comments by expressing a fear that he may have been waffling. He then makes a few more comments about using mathematics, mainly in the context of shopping. His rather sad conclusion states that he has always seen himself as a failure at calculating.

## Wendy's story

The final writer to be considered was an 80 year old woman with two daughters and one granddaughter. She described herself as a retired primary teacher. Wendy starts her account by describing a family card game and her first paragraph is reproduced in full below. This was followed by short mentions of shopping and of calculators. Wendy then returned to the subject of her granddaughter and subsequently related this to her own primary education. The paragraphs concerned are given below.

By coincidence, when considering this directive and its first part, we had our small family with us over Easter. As usual, we played card games. The family consisted of myself, husband, two daughters (e.50 years) and 11 year old granddaughter Julia. Such games always involve keeping scores and, from being 4 years old, Julia has always kept a keen eye on these – checking that the scorer – usually grandpa – has got it correct! On this occasion, he began to show Julia how to add up columns of four numbers. Elizabeth, our elder daughter, joined in, but our younger daughter, Kate, and I, did not. We are sufficiently numerate to cope with shopping, bank statements etc. but otherwise, numbers do not enthral us. My father loves numerical puzzles and tried to help us with maths homework, but my sister and I found it very difficult. Not until I became a primary school teacher did I really understand the fact that $^5/_{10}$ ths was a half! This in spite of having gained a credit in maths in school certificate (forerunner of GCEs!) However, Kate can often beat her father at cribbage- a game involving numbers!...

I remember taking my four year old granddaughter to infant school in East London a few weeks before Christmas. She suddenly stopped and asked 'Granny, how many days will it be before Father Christmas comes?' My 7 times table supplied an instant answer. 'But Granny, how could you have the answer so quickly?' replied Julia. 'Easy', I said, 'when you know your tables!'

When I moved from infant school to junior school, the school day lasted a half hour longer. In that half term the extra time was spent practising our tables. Teacher drew a large clock face on the blackboard and wrote a number from one to twelve in the centre. She would then point to a time on the clock and we would call out the answer. (Wendy, age 80)

Wendy finished her account by discussing mathematics used in the home, in particular the weighing of cookery ingredients and her recollections of being given her first pair of scales.

## What can we learn from Henry and Wendy?

Both Henry and Wendy mention mathematical activity carried out jointly by grandparents and grandchildren. In Wendy's case, the mathematics arises in the context of a game, though it appears that this opportunity is being used to introduce some new mathematics rather than just to practice. The account also suggests that this is a regular activity and that the child was motivated to do the calculations in order to check that her grandpa is scoring correctly. The mathematics in this case involves three generations working together. Playing games of this type may be seen as a key opportunity for children to use mathematics alongside their families and is one of the types of activity reported on by the Basic Skills Agency in a project concerning learning with grandparents (Al-Azami, 2006).

In Henry's case, the mathematics in question is the homework set for the children. Henry appears to be engaged in this and to understand how it can be difficult for children. It also seems that he uses the experience of helping with homework to reconsider the mathematics he was taught and the reasons for learning it. Wendy raises the issue of learning tables following a discussion with her granddaughter on the way to school. Like Henry, she makes the connection between the current event and her own experience as a learner.

Wendy's account also contains a brief mention of her role as a primary teacher when she suggests that she only really understood equivalent fractions when she came to teach them. Both Kate and Henry show that they have revisited and rethought their ideas about school mathematics throughout their lives. They have had opportunities to do this as grand-parents and, in Wendy's case, as a teacher. This contrasts with the experience of some of the other writers, who appear to have a fixed view of primary mathematics that has not changed since they were at school. A related issue is that some of the writers who have had no recent contact with schools have developed inaccurate and sometimes over-critical views of current practice in mathematics teaching (Houssart, 2006, 2007), something which Henry and Wendy have avoided.

These two accounts suggest that, in some families at least, grand-parents play a role in mathematical learning. This is consistent with other work suggesting that many grandparents have an active role in caring for children (Buchanan *et al*, 2008)). Recent advice (Williams, 2008) stresses the importance of being aware of the role of families in mathematical learning. One aspect of this role is the impression families transmit to children of the part mathematics plays in everyday life. In Henry and Wendy's cases, the grandchildren apparently receive positive messages in this respect. Another issue is that teachers need to recognise the mathematical knowledge picked up outside the classroom and make links between this out-of-school mathematics and that learned in school (Williams, 2008, p70). The addition of cribbage scores by Julia and her family presents an ideal example of this and it is interesting to note the similarity with the house game discussed by Hilary Evens in an earlier chapter.

## What are the implications of these findings?

For those working in primary education, perhaps the most striking aspect of these findings is that many writers discuss their experiences at primary school when asked about the mathematics they currently do. Although clear dangers exist in generalising from these findings, it seems that, for some learners at least, attitudes to mathematics formed at primary school tend to persist. It is encouraging that so many of these older people have positive memories of the mathematics they learned at school. This contrasts with studies which report more negative feelings (eg Buxton, 1981) and with the received wisdom amongst some in mathematics education that a focus on mental arithmetic and speedy recall of number facts has left some with fear and loathing of mathematics.

The findings also suggest that grandparents can play a role in their grandchildren's mathematical learning and perhaps there is potential for schools to show greater recognition of this. In addition to the Williams report, an Ofsted (2007) document also highlights the positive contribution grandparents can make to schools. In addition to their motivational role, the report gives examples of grandparents contributing to the history, literacy, geography and religious education curricula. We suggest that grandparents might also play a role in sharing their own experiences of learning and using mathematics. Crucially, this potentially becomes a two-way process, showing older people how mathematics is currently taught, assisting them in helping their grandchildren and dispelling the myth that the subject is no longer given priority.

The findings also have implications beyond primary education. For those working in adult education, particularly with older adults, they suggest the contours of a range of attitudes held by at least some. For those interested in older people's welfare, the finding that some respondents appear to be doing mathematics not for functional reasons but for reasons of leisure or even mental agility may be of interest. Much is said about enabling people to remain physically and mentally active later in their lives and it may be that mathematics has a part to play in this.

## References

Al-Azami (2006) *The Silver Lining of my Life, Learning with Grandparents: A report of the work of the National Development Project 2005-2006 funded by the Basic Skills Agency*, London: The Basic Skills Agency

Bloome, D, Sheridan, D, Street, B (1993) *Reading Mass-Observation Writing: Theoretical and Methodological Issues in Researching the Mass-Observation Archive*, (Mass-Observation Archive, Occasional Paper Number 1). University of Sussex: Mass-Observation Archive

Brown, M (2001) Influences on the teaching of number in England. In J. Anghileri (ed) *Principles and Practices in Arithmetic Teaching*. Buckingham: Open University Press

Buchanan, A, Flouri, E, Tan, J-P, Griggs, J and Attar-Achwartz, S (2008) Grandparenting: the growing influence of grandparents. *Child RIGHT* 248 p14-18

Buxton, L (1981) *Do You Panic about Maths? Coping with Maths Anxiety*, London: Heinemann Educational

Crook, J and Briggs, M (1991) Bags and baggage. In D. Pimm and E. Love (eds) *Teaching and Learning School Mathematics*. London: Hodder and Stoughton

Houssart, J (2006) The views of older adults on school mathematics past and present. *British Society for Research into Learning Mathematics*, Proceedings of the Day Conference held at the University of Warwick, Saturday 25th February 2006

Houssart, J (2007) They don't use their brains, what a pity: School mathematics through the eyes of the older generation. *Research in Mathematics Education* Volume 9, p47-63

Munn, P (1997) Children's beliefs about counting. In I. Thompson (ed) *Teaching and Learning Early Number.* Buckingham: Open University Press

Ofsted (2007) *Parents, Carers and Schools.* (reference number 070018, July 2007) London: OFSTED Publications

Sheridan, D (1996) *Damned Anecdotes and Dangerous Confabulations: mass-observation as life history*, (Mass-Observation Archive, Occasional Paper Number 7). University of Sussex: Mass-Observation Archive

Williams, P (2008) *Independent Review of Mathematics Teaching in Early Years Settings and Primary Schools: Final Reports.* Nottingham: DCSF Publications

# 12

## Learning from listening to yourself

### *John Mason*

### Introduction

Learning mathematics can be supported by providing opportunities for learners to manipulate familiar objects to get a sense of relationships which are instances of important properties such as mathematical concepts and facts. Through doing, talking and attempting to record, they can work towards articulating those concepts and facts. Learners rarely reach articulation at their first attempt, however. They scramble words, hesitate in the middle of saying something, and resort to particular instances or cases. This is all part of the process. Important things happen as learners try to reconstruct for themselves, in their own words and in conventional terms, what they are coming to understand.

In order to support learning, it helps to sensitise yourself to learners' struggles: really useful to be reminded of what that struggle is like and the best way to do this is to challenge yourself mathematically by placing yourself in a similar situation and become a learner again. When groups of teachers work together on mathematics – be it on explorations related to work they will later offer their learners or on tasks only indirectly related to the curriculum – they can support each other and pay attention to each others' struggles to articulate understanding. It is also valuable to work for and by yourself every so often to experience that feeling of being stuck: this is an honourable state and one to be celebrated, not regretted: only when you get stuck on something can you appreciate what eventually gets you unstuck.

This chapter suggests some tactics which a teacher can use to go beyond the now commonplace claim that it is good for learners to discuss things together. The chapter takes as its data the experiences which come up for readers when they engage in some of the tasks proposed here. It offers examples of challenges through which you can listen to yourself. The tasks are accompanied by personal accounts of work on these tasks, which form an analysis of the data to the extent that you recognise what is described as consonant or dissonant with your own experience. By participating in this way, you become aware of opportunities to prompt learners to work in this way.

## Watch What You Do

Watch What You Do, or WWYD for short, turns out to be a useful way for the head to listen to what the body has to say, in order to see a generality through the particular. The task below can also be found in Mason, Johnston-Wilder and Graham (2005, p282), and Mason (1998).

## Task 1: Shady Circles

In the first block of circles below, quickly shade in every third dot starting from the second, counting from left to right and continuing the count from row to row.

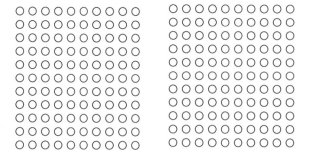

Pay attention to how you do it.

In the second block, shade in every seventh starting from the third.

## *Account*

When I first did this task, I started off counting then shading, counting then shading. Suddenly I noticed a slight change of pace. My speed increased and my body took over and followed the pattern being made by the shaded dots. I realised that I had actually stopped counting. My head soon intervened and wanted to know if this was correct and so I went back to some counting in order to check, but soon I was back shading according to the perceived pattern.

This task can only be effective if you are able to listen to yourself, to be sensitive to a shift of initiative from head to body, from cognition to enaction. By paying attention to what your body has become aware of, you can become intellectually aware of patterns that might be exploited, explored, developed and justified mathematically. This experience and a number of others like it led to the teaching tactic called Watch What You Do.

Young children are able to generalise, because without it they could not function in the world and certainly could not grasp language.

## Task 2: Threaks

A young child, on encountering a fish-fork with only three tines, asked 'is this a threak'? What might have prompted this question?

A young child, sitting in a highchair after a visit to a canal a short distance away announced 'if the canal rises our feet will get wet'. What might the child have been thinking?

## *Account*

At first I was a bit thrown, and then suddenly I realised that it is highly likely that the first child associated the word *fork* with the number four because of the same sound as a homonym. I have deliberately spelled the child's word as *threak* rather than threek or 3*k* so as not to make the connection so obvious. *Threak* can be interpreted as an example of a young child generalising using the name as the number of tines with a *k* on the end, without knowing the word *tine*. Presumably one could test this by offering five or six tines, but notice the subtlety in discrimination: knives are not confused with *wunks* or *oneks*!

I was struck by the reasoning implicit in the second child's assertion, and the degree of generality it contains: water rising by no specified amount and a fantastical scenario. Presumably he had a moment of insight, possibly connected with being put in a highchair so that his feet were off the ground. Perhaps he had a sense of the water in the canal rising but not reaching his feet immediately because he had been lifted off the floor. If so, it suggests a complexity of awarenesses and thoughts triggered by routine actions carried out by adults.

Children often mistake homonyms, so it is worth being alert to potential confusions when introducing new words in mathematics, but here the added component is the generalisation from four to other numbers. A really useful exercise when working with young children is to keep a notebook in which you record instances of generalisations and other reasoning. The fact of the notebook and your desire to record such utterances helps to sharpen your observation, and sharpened perception leads to new and motivating discoveries. The point is to develop an appreciation of the powers of young children to generalise and to reason.

## Task 3: Different differences

Ask someone to think of a three digit number, and someone else to think of a two digit number. Just before you ask them for their numbers so that you can find their difference (subtracting smaller from larger), someone else says 'let's add one to both their numbers'. What difference will it make to the difference?

### Account

I have a penchant for making questions more difficult by using unusual words or the same word with a slightly different meaning. I do this because it challenges me to work on interpreting the question, and sensitises me to subtle differences in the way that words are used: hence different differences.

I saw immediately that adding 1 to both could make no difference because of my deeply ingrained sense of difference as the gap between the numbers which is unchanged by adding one to both. For me this is linked to my sense of subtraction but subtraction may not trigger that link in learners. It is a bodily-based awareness which is formalised in mathematics as the root of children's own methods for subtracting multi-digit numbers.

Here the important feature is that it makes no difference: adding 1 to both numbers leaves the gap or difference between them invariant and this is an example of a pervasive theme in mathematics: invariance in the midst of change. The difference in the differences is unchanged by adding one to both numbers. More importantly, an assertion can be made about the difference in the differences even though we do not know what the actual numbers are! The difference in the differences remains invariant when the original numbers are changed. This is again an example of a generality, a statement which is true for any two numbers. The task is proposed vaguely with no mention of the numbers in order to highlight the possibility of reasoning about unknown numbers, something that young children can also do.

With any question it is useful to ask yourself 'what can I change and still the answer will be the same?' and 'what can I change and still the method will be the same?' For example here, the 1 which is to be added to both numbers could be changed to any number, and it could be subtracted from both numbers rather than added to them. The task can be extended further, by adding or subtracting different numbers. Thus, 'If we add 1 to the larger and add 2 to the smaller, what will be the difference in the differences?' can still be answered even though we do not know the original numbers: the answer 'it will be 1 less than the original difference' is independent of the original numbers – it is invariant when the numbers themselves are changed.

## Task 4: Decimal descent
Chant out loud, the numbers you get by starting at 100 and subtracting 1.1 each time.

### Account
The first time I did this I paused over the first number, 98.9, to make sure I was not making a silly mistake. The following numbers were easy and I got into a nice rhythm, only to be interrupted by 90.1 and catching myself making a mistake by carrying on the pattern! This reminded me of other situations in which, once a pattern is established, routine takes over and thinking stops. This can also happen all too easily for learners doing repetitive tasks.

This task works best in a group where you try to keep up the speed. There are places where the pace slows down, then speeds up again and gradually the slowing down gets shorter and shorter as confidence and insight grows.

The experience is a lovely example of how our bodies detect patterns and our thinking follows, until suddenly our thinking is needed again. This is another example of the power to detect and act upon patterns which all humans possess and which can be exercised and developed through mathematics.

Features which can be altered in the task include the starting value for example, 1000, and the decimal value being subtracted, for example 1.01, 11, 1.5, ... The idea for the next task comes from Pat Thompson (2002).

## Task 4: Fractional parts

As you gaze at the figure, ask yourself if you can see:

> Something which is 2/5 of something else;
> Something which is 3/5 of something else;
> Something which is 2/3 of something else;
> Something which is 5/2 of something else;
> Something which is 5/3 of something else;
> Something which is 3/2 of something else;

### Account

The first time I came across this task I quickly dealt with the first two and then found myself stumbling slightly as I searched for a two-ness and a three-ness, and then realised that one need not be an actual part, just the same size as, a part of the other. From there I found myself enjoying looking out for relationships to instantiate the actions of the fractional operators.

The first two are familiar, perhaps, but the third often causes concern. Perhaps people expect the part to be a part of the whole rather than the same size as a part of the whole. Indeed a more complete statement might be 'the shaded squares are the same as two-thirds of the un-shaded squares'. How do you break out of 'I can't see it'? At first I am trapped in my expectation that the whole being sought is the whole of the diagram. Once released from that assumption, more is possible!

The third requires that you alter what the whole is of which you are then identifying a potential same-sized part. This highlights the fact that a fraction is an operator so that it is necessary to be clear what the unit or the whole is, on which the fraction the operates. This task not only introduces a core awareness concerning fractions but also offers an opportunity to trap the movement of attention needed in order to find different wholes on which to operate.

## Task 4A: More fractional parts

Now, in the same diagram, try to see:

> 2/5 of 5/2 of something;
> 3/5 of 5/3 of something; generalise!
> 1 ÷ 2/5 of something;
> 1 ÷ 3/5 of something;
> 3/5 ÷ 2/5 of something;
> 2/5 ÷ 3/5 of something;

### Account

I noticed that I was imposing my own extra colouring, in stressing some parts and allowing others to go into the background, in order to see something. Stressing, and consequently ignoring, leads to generalisation.

Compound fractions require choosing something appropriate to attend to so that the first operator's effect can be seen, and then acting the second operator on that. The final step involves recognising the result. In some cases it is the thing you started with; in others it is the same size as a fraction of some other whole. These movements of attention are vital in order to fully appreciate what fractions are about. Developing facility in choosing what to attend to benefits not just the learning of fractions but of mathematics and of many other subjects as well.

Tackling a more complicated figure such as the following leads to an even more open and challenging task:

## Task 4B: Even more fractional parts

What fractional operators can you discern in the shading in this diagram?

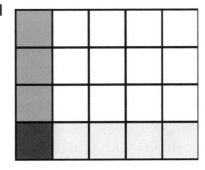

## Account

The first time I used this with colleagues, I suddenly realised that there are related tasks, such as counting the number of different ways of seeing one group as a given fraction of some other group. Furthermore I could see equivalences such as $\frac{4}{16}$ and $\frac{1}{4}$, and $1 - \frac{8}{20}$ and $\frac{12}{20}$.

I found myself seeing $\frac{1}{4}$ of $\frac{1}{5}$ and $\frac{1}{5}$ of $\frac{1}{4}$; also $\frac{3}{4}$ of $\frac{4}{5}$ and $\frac{4}{5}$ of $\frac{3}{4}$; and so on.

I also found myself seeing $\frac{1}{4} - \frac{1}{5} = \frac{1}{20}$, and then realised that I could look through the diagram to see an $n$ by $n+1$ grid with $1/n - 1/n+1 = 1/n(n+1)$. What happens to your other seeings if the grid is $n$ by $n + 1$, or even $n$ by $m$?

This task provides an opportunity to challenge each other in finding less and less prominent uses of fractions as operators, and exploring operators acting on the results of operators acting on ...

## What we learn from listening to ourselves

The proposal is that when and if the slogan Watch What You Do comes to mind, it can remind you to pause and pay attention to what your body is suggesting in the way of patterns and relationships: this can help you see through the particular to a generality. More subtly, watching how your attention moves about, counting subgroups and relating them to other subgroups affords insight into the demands on learners encountering such tasks for the first time. The reason this is important and valuable is that most mathematics concerns generality. Even to do elementary arithmetic you need to use general principles, such as that addition and multiplication are commutative, that subtraction and division are not; that dividing by zero is unwise. Dave Hewitt (1998) makes the case eloquently that mastery of arithmetic depends on algebraic thinking. You do not need to be consciously aware that you are using general principles, though if you are it helps you to catch your mistakes.

It is also possible to use a variant of WWYD, namely Say What You See to overcome initial reactions to complexity. By announcing features which strike you, and by listening to features which strike other people, you can clarify and enrich your thinking. By working on individual components you can piece together what the whole complexity is telling you.

By listening to yourself, by watching what you do, and by saying what you see, you can become more aware of details within complex situations, of patterns and relationships which may be instances of more general properties than is evident at first. In a sense you are opening yourself up to mathematical structure, allowing your perceptual apparatus to offer up data which can be used by your natural powers to make sense of mathematics and to make mathematical sense of the material world.

## Using SWYS and WWYD

Here are two final task domains for which listening to yourself, and also listening to what the mathematical structure is trying to say to you, can lead to pleasurable success in appreciating underlying mathematical structure.

The next task was, I believe, first published by Alistair Macintosh and Douglas Quadling (1975). It was popular in the 1980s, and re-popularised in a simplistic form in the National Strategy of 1999, without making explicit the real potential for its use in exposing and developing mathematical thinking. If you are already familiar with arithmogons, try the arithmogon variant, because the purpose of these tasks is to get yourself into a position where you can listen to yourself as you work and gain insight into the sorts of struggles learners might have.

## Task 5 Arithmogons

Doing: in the first diagram, the numbers in the squares are to be the sums of the numbers on either end of the line.

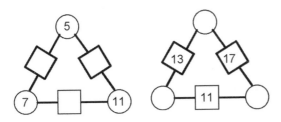

Undoing: given the numbers in the boxes, find which numbers could have been in the circles.

## Comment

Guess and check, perhaps developed into guess, check and adjust, is certainly one approach. However, if you kept running into arithmogons with different entries in the squares, much as an entrepreneur might keep having customers asking for particular packages ... then just as the entrepreneur needs a general policy, you would soon want a general method, or even a general formula for answering all such arithmogon questions. So you need something more than a solution to this particular instance.

The arithmogon given could be a bit of a shock because there are no integer solutions. A sensible thing to do if nothing else comes to mind is to make up your own simpler arithmogons, which is a form of specialising, perhaps at first starting with the circle numbers, then trying to see relationships between the square and the circle numbers. Once you begin to see some relationships, you can Watch What You Do as you solve one of your own, where you know the answer, in order to get a sense of what to do in general. What sorts of numbers guarantee whole number entries in the circles?

If you are familiar and confident with algebra, then you could 'acknowledge your ignorance' of what values fit in the circles, denote one of them by a cloud or a letter such as $V$ and then proceed to Say What You See concerning the facts about the figure-making use of your $V$. This notion of acknowledging ignorance was a favourite phrase used by Mary Boole for initiating algebra (Tahta, 1972). By denoting the fact of your ignorance as to the value, you have an object, which may be a symbol, to treat as if it were the number, so that you can construct expressions as if you were doing arithmetic. Placing a $V$ in the upper circle forces the lower circles to be $13 - V$ and $17 - V$ respectively, and these have to add up to 11. But this is a full-frontal approach which is less efficient that recognising relationships that have to hold. For example you could consider the sum of the numbers in the squares.

## Task 5A: Arithmogon variant

How could you assign numbers to the vertices of a die so that the sum of the vertex numbers around a face gives the value on that face? Note that the 6 is the sum of the four outside circles.

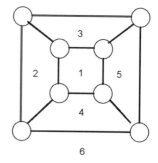

## Comment

A sensible thing to do first might be to try a single quadrilateral version of an arithmogon, to see what is going on, then extend to more quadrilaterals glued together. No one said there had to be a unique solution ... so a typical move is to impose an extra condition. Is there a solution with all the vertex numbers positive?

Effective specialising is not always easy to spot. Did you think of trying $1/4$ for each of the vertices summing 1, and then building up from there for the faces summing to 2, 3, 4 and 5? Why does the sixth face work if the others all work?

Did you think of trying a tetrahedron instead of a cube? It more closely resembles the original arithmogon! This might encourage you to try an octahedron, icosohedron, or even a dodecahedron.

This challenging variant suggests various ways in which arithmogons can be varied and extended. Triangles can be fitted together along their edges, other polygons can be used, multiplication could replace addition and you could have mixed arithmogons with addition and multiplication! If the edges had directions, then you could use subtraction and division as well.

A related task that is popular is the following:

## Task 5B: Pyramids

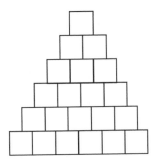

Each number is the sum of the numbers below it. How few entries must you provide so as to determine the pyramid completely? In how many different ways can you specify this number and still the pyramid is uniquely determined?

## Comment

The bottom row provides a doing task, since each row above is then determined. But what if you are given the top entry: which other entries are needed to force a single solution? Having chosen positions for starting values, provide a formula for each of the other entries.

Again a sensible way to start is to build your own, and to watch What You Do as you fill in cells so as to get a sense of how it works. Then try rubbing out entries you think you can deduce. You might also start with smaller pyramids but then generalise to larger ones.

The operation of adding could be replaced. For example, each cell could be the one below to the right subtracted from the one below to the left. How is this one related to the original task?

Addition could also be replaced by multiplication, and subtraction by division.

A move into three dimensions is possible, with cubes stacked in tetrahedral so each layer is triangular as shown below.

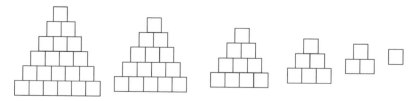

Again, Say What You See is helpful in working your way into the task, discerning details, recognising relationships, and perceiving properties that might apply in general.

## Task 6: Discerning shapes

In the picture, can you discern a right-angled triangle? How many? How many parallelograms? How many kites and darts? Describe to someone else one of the shapes you are seeing, without using your hands to point. Perhaps they are looking at the picture but on the other end of a telephone!

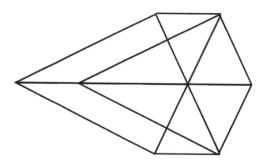

*Account*

I found it useful to do this with colleagues: each person picks out a shape and then challenges others to see it. It is sort of the reverse of Say What You See, because you challenge others to See What You See!

Discerning subfigures is a crucial activity before it is possible to think coherently geometrically. Tasks like this afford opportunity to work on visual acuity and on describing briefly but vividly how to see what you are seeing.

## Conclusion

Through offering accounts of tackling mathematical problems, the strategies of Say What You See and Watch What You Do emerge from listening to myself as learner. As pedagogic strategies, they can be used explicitly to encourage learners to listen to themselves as learners. If over time the overt reference to them becomes less and less direct, and more indirect , such as 'what did you do last time in a situation with a diagram, set of exercises, confusing formula ...?', learners can be encouraged to internalise these strategies, and so to listen to themselves as learners, while working on mathematics. The process of gradually changing direct prompts into indirect prompts so that eventually learners spontaneously use the strategy for themselves was labelled *directed-prompted-spontaneous* in an OU course Floyd *et al* (1981) and was called *scaffolding and fading* by Brown *et al* (1989). When teachers fade their initial scaffolding, students can improve their problem solving and thinking skills through being sensitised to strategies they can choose to use for themselves, not just within mathematics. The use by learners of their own natural powers to imagine and express relationships and generalities is a source of inspiration and contributes to the growth of self-esteem. By opening themselves to mathematical structure they may find themselves appreciating the material world more fully, and finding themselves in a more powerful position to pursue their personal interests in the future.

## References

Brown, S, Collins, A and Duguid, P (1989) Situated Cognition and the Culture of Learning. *Educational Researcher* 18 (1) p32-41

Floyd, A, Burton, L, James, N and Mason, J (1981) *EM235: Developing Mathematical Thinking.* Milton Keynes: Open University

Hewitt, D (1998) Approaching Arithmetic Algebraically. *Mathematics Teaching* 163 pp19-29

Macintosh, A and Quadling, D (1975) Arithmogons. *Mathematics Teaching* 70 pp18-23

Mason, J (1998) *Learning and Doing Mathematics* (Second revised edition). York: QED Books

Mason, J with Johnston-Wilder, S and Graham, A (2005) *Developing Thinking in Algebra*. London: Sage (Paul Chapman)

Tahta, D (1972) *A Boolean Anthology: selected writings of Mary Boole on mathematics education*. Derby: Association of Teachers of Mathematics

Thompson, P (2002) Didactic Objects and Didactic Models in Radical Constructivism. In K. Gravemeijer, R. Lehrer, B. van Oers, L. Verschaffel (eds), *Symbolizing, Modeling, and Tool Use in Mathematics Education*. Dordrecht, The Netherlands: Kluwer

# Notes on contributors

**Nichola Abraham** was born and brought up in Trinidad. She has recently worked in London with children between two and four years old. She is currently embarking on postgraduate study in child development and has a particular interest in children's early mathematical development.

**Barbara Allen** is director of the Centre for Mathematics Education at the Open University. Her research interests include attitudes to learning mathematics and the professional development of mathematics teachers. She has also researched pupils' perceptions of mathematics classrooms.

**Mary Briggs** is an Associate Professor in the Institute of Education at the University of Warwick. She teaches on a number of different education courses with a specific research interest in mathematics education. She has worked in a wide range of settings, including children's homes, special, primary schools and universities.

**Brian Dale** is currently studying to become a primary teacher at university. He has been working in a primary school in Islington for the last four years. His interests include watching live bands play, cinema, travelling and Pilates.

**Roger Duke** has worked in the School of Information Technology at the University of Queensland since 1989. Before that he worked for ten years in the Mathematics Department at the Open University. His current research interest is in the creation of computer software to help teach mathematical concepts.

**Hilary Evens** has worked on mathematics with all ages from very young children to over eighties, though most of her time was spent as a teacher in secondary schools. She has also been a researcher, writer and lecturer in the Centre for Mathematics Education at the Open University.

**Alan Graham** works at the Open University's Centre for Mathematics Education, writing courses in mathematics education and mathematics. Before that he was a school teacher for five years. His professional interests are in teaching statistics and using ICT, particularly graphics calculators and computer applets, to excite and inspire learners.

**Dr Dave Hewitt** is currently a Senior Lecturer at the University of Birmingham, having taught previously in several secondary schools. He has two daughters from whom he has learnt so much over the years and is a governor of their primary school.

**Jenny Houssart** has a background in primary teaching. She is currently Senior Lecturer at the Institute of Education, London, where she works on a range of undergraduate and postgraduate courses. She has a particular research interest in children considered to be low attainers in primary mathematics.

**Andreas O Kyriakides** is a primary school teacher in Cyprus and is also pursuing a PhD in mathematics education at the Open University, UK. He is interested in working with diagrams as a productive basis for students to reconstruct, explore and expand their mathematics knowledge.

**John Mason** is Professor of Mathematics Education at the Open University's Centre for Mathematics education and Senior Research Fellow at the University of Oxford. He has written and co-written a large number of books, articles and chapters on mathematics education as well as contributing to many Open University courses.

**Elizabeth Ryder** is a Teaching Assistant, working in a primary school in South-East London while completing a Foundation Degree at the Institute of Education, University of London. Prior to embarking on a career in education she was a Stage Manager at the National Theatre, South Bank, London.

**Lisa Strong** became a Teaching Assistant nine years ago, returning to work after having two children. She works primarily with children with special educational needs in a mainstream school. She is currently in the second year of a foundation degree and enjoys the challenges that being a mature student bring.

# Author Index

Ainley, J 15
Al-Azami, S 152, 154
Allen, B 123, 125
Arksey, H 103, 114
Arnot, M 64, 69
Askew, M 125
Attar-Achwartz, S 44,154
Aubrey, C 56, 57

Ball, S 67, 69
Bauersfeld, H 60, 69
Billington, T 59, 69
Bills, L 15
Bloome, D 144, 154
Boaler, J 116, 119, 125
Briggs, M 55, 57, 143,
  154
Brissenden, T 60, 69
Brown, L 15
Brown, M 146, 154
Brown, S 169
Bruner, J 72, 73, 74, 82,
  84
Buchanan, A 43, 44, 153,
  154
Burton, L 169
Buxton, L 143, 153, 154

Clark, A ii, x, 18, 20, 28,
  29
Cobb, P 60, 70
Cohen, L 123, 126
Coles, A 15

Collins, A 169
Commission on the
  Future of Multi-Ethnic
  Britain 64, 70
Coulthard, M 60, 70
Crook, J 143, 154

Dahl, S 56, 57
Davis, B vii, xi, 87, 99
Department for Children,
  Schools and Families
  24, 29
Dimattia, C 99
Dockett, S 48, 57
Doerr, H. M. 90, 98, 99
Dowker, A 34, 44
Duguid, P 169
Duke, R 71, 84
Dunphy, E 18, 24, 29
Duveen, G 69

EMAS 139, 142
Emblen, V 140, 142
Evans, J 18, 29
Even, R viii, xi
Evens, H 102, 114

Flouri, E 43, 44, 154
Floyd, A 169
Fuller, M 67, 70
Fuson, K 133, 142

Gallistel, C 137, 139, 142
Gattegno, C 41, 44
Gelman, R 137, 139, 142
Gifford, S 22, 24, 28, 29,
  42, 44
Ginsburg, H 56, 57
Glaser, B 115, 126
Graham, A 71, 75, 84,
  102, 114, 158, 170
Graham, L 75, 84
Gray, J 69
Gregory, R 116, 126
Griggs, J 44, 154
Griffiths, R 21, 29, 135,
  137, 140, 142

Hewitt, D 15, 42, 44, 164,
  169
Heyman, R 86, 99
Houssart, J 62, 67, 69,
  70, 102, 114, 153, 155
Hoyles, C 72, 84
Hughes, M 36, 44

Ifrah, G 137, 140, 141,
  142
Issit, J viii, xi

James, M 69
James, N 169
Johnston-Wilder, S 84,
  102, 114, 158, 170

Kaplan, M 141, 142
Kenner, C 137, 142
Knight, P 103, 114
Kwon, Y 133, 142
Kyriacou, C viii, xi

Land, F 137, 142
Lara-Meloy, T 99
Lee, B 126

Macintosh, A 165, 169
Maclellan, E 41, 44
Manion, L 123, 126
Mason, J 5, 15, 86, 95,
    98, 99, 102, 114, 158,
    169, 170
McLeod, A viii, xi
Maxwell, B 86, 99
Menninger, K 133, 136,
    142
Munn, P 20, 21, 22, 24,
    29, 34, 35, 44, 149,
    155
Moss, P x, xi, 18, 20, 28,
    29

NALDIC 131, 142
Nemirovsky, R 86, 99

Office for Standards in
    Education 116, 126,
    154, 155

Paechter, C 123, 126
Perry, B 48, 57
Pomerantz, M 59, 69

Quadling, D 165, 169

Radice, W 136, 142
Ramani, G 38, 44
Ravet, J 59, 70
Riberio, B 99
Richards, J 60, 70
Rinaldi, C viii, xi
Roberts-Holmes, G 18,
    28, 29
Rogers, S 18, 29
Rudduck, J 69

Salmon, K 56, 57
Sewell, T 67, 70
Sharratt, N 39, 44
Sheridan, D 144, 154,
    155
Siegler, R 38, 44
Sinclair, J 60, 70
Skemp, R 49, 57
Slavin, R 116, 126
Strauss 115, 126
Street, B 144, 154
Sukhnandan, L 116, 126

Tahta, D 166, 170
Tan, J-P 44, 154
Thompson, P 162, 170
Tripp, J 90, 98, 99

Voigt, J 60, 70

Wallach, T viii, xi
Watson, A 9, 15
Webb, R 124, 126
Wenger, E 122, 126
Wesson, M 56, 57
Williams, P viii, xi, 39, 44,
    126, 153, 155
Willis, P 67, 70
Wilson, K 15

Yackel, E 60, 70

# Subject Index

activities 8, 24, 32, 34-35, 38, 39, 42, 43, 44, 45, 46, 56, 86, 140, 145
*see also* tasks
addition 8, 15, 53, 64, 65, 85-88, 96-98, 145, 164, 167-168
algebra 15, 71-84, 101-102, 164, 166
angles 8, 63
arithmogons 165-167
assessment 24-28,34-38, 49-50, 53, 68, 106-108, 117, 124, 145
authority 67, 92, 117, 119, 120, 123-125

calculator 24, 61, 146, 151
camera 18-29
carers 22, 24, 29, 35
classroom assistant 60, 68 *see also* teaching assistant
classroom discussion 54-56, 61, 68-69, 89-96, 113-114
classroom observation 32, 50-52, 60-66, 87-96
classroom organisation 52, 113-114, 121-123

counting
    counting activities 31-34, 40-41, 145-149, 150, 158-159, 164
    counting in different languages 127-142
    principles of counting 135, 137, 139
    purpose of counting 20-21, 24, 34-35, 46-49
    *see also* number
Cyprus 85-100

decimals 14-15, 145, 161-162
denominator 87-97, 151
division 13,145, 150, 164, 167, 168

equations 72, 75-84

family 21, 31-44, 133-134, 136, 138, 140, 149, 153, 157
fractions 9, 19, 63, 66, 74-75, 85-100, 151, 152, 162-164

games 24, 32, 36-43, 147-149, 151-152
grandparents 36, 43, 149-154

grounded theory 115
grouping and attainment 52-53
    *see also* setting

home
home-school links17, 39
observations at home 1-3, 5-6, 10, 37

intergenerational learning 43
interviews 18-24, 28, 46-50, 56-57, 77-84, 101-114, 115-124

learning modes 72-74

Mass-Observation archive 143-144
measurement 32, 36, 145-146
measuring area 4
    measuring capacity 50-53
    measuring perimeter 14-15
    *See also* units
mental mathematics 53, 63-64, 75, 82-83, 144-149, 153-154
misconceptions 52-54

mosaic approach 18-24, 28-29
multiplication 61, 72, 91-96, 145-146, 164, 167, 168

negative numbers 6-8, 64
number
  beliefs about numbers 19-24
  Bengali numbers 133-138
  big numbers 11
  Chinese-based number systems 133
  European number systems 133
  French numbers 132-133
  German numbers 128-133
  number lines 23, 139
numbers in the environment 19-24
origin of number systems 132-133, 137-138, 140-141
Tamil numbers 138-141
see also counting, decimals, fractions

parents 1-15, 20, 22, 24, 31-43
place value 33, 140
practical maths , 43, 52-53, 55, 64, 74-75, 145, 148-149
problems 9-10, 12-13, 42, 54, 56, 71, 74, 76-84, 101-102, 107-108, 111-112, 150, 151-169
pupil perspectives 18, 48, 115-126
puzzles 146-147, 151

questioning 8-10, 28, 35, 50, 53, 59-60, 98

role of adults 42-43, 52-53

setting 59, 66, 115-126
  see also grouping and attainment
shape 24-28, 32, 36, 168-169
shopping 10-11, 38-39, 146, 148, 150-151
subtraction 8, 61, 63, 64, 72, 76, 79-82, 105, 110, 145, 160-161, 164, 167-168

tables 62, 145, 151-152
  see also multiplication
tasks 3-4, 14-15, 42, 45, 52-56, 64, 73-77, 83, 86-87, 112, 141,157-169 see also activities
teachers 17, 22, 24, 49, 54-56, 66-68, 73, 84, 86, 98, 106, 113, 116-117, 121-125, 133, 136, 148, 149, 151-152, 157, 169
teaching assistants see classroom assistants
technology 2, 71-84, 88, 92-95, 100

units 10-13, 50, 62, 69, 145-146, 150 see also measurement

using and applying mathematics 144-147

written accounts 53-54, 97-98, 104-113, 143, 145-148, 150-152